MATT AND TOM OLDFIELD

ULTIMATE
FOOTBALL HEROES

FODEN

FROM THE PLAYGROUND
TO THE PITCH

DINO

First published by Dino Books in 2022,
an imprint of Bonnier Books UK,
4th Floor, Victoria House, Bloomsbury Square, London WC1B 4DA
Owned by Bonnier Books,
Sveavägen 56, Stockholm, Sweden

🐦 @UFHbooks
📷 @footieheroesbks
www.heroesfootball.com
www.bonnierbooks.co.uk

Design by www.envydesign.co.uk

Paperback ISBN: 978 1 78946 572 3
E-book ISBN: 978 1 78946 573 0

British Library cataloguing-in-publication data:
A catalogue record for this book is available from the British Library.

Printed and bound in Great Britain by Clays Ltd, Elcograf S.p.A.

1 3 5 7 9 10 8 6 4 2

MIX
Paper from
responsible sources
FSC® C018072

For all readers,
young and old(er)

ULTIMATE
FOOTBALL HEROES

Matt Oldfield is an accomplished writer and the editor-in-chief
of football review site Of Pitch & Page. Tom Oldfield is a
freelance sports writer and the author of biographies on
Cristiano Ronaldo, Arsène Wenger and Rafael Nadal.

Cover illustration by Dan Leydon.
To learn more about Dan visit danleydon.com
To purchase his artwork visit etsy.com/shop/footynews
Or just follow him on Twitter @danleydon

TABLE OF CONTENTS

ACKNOWLEDGEMENTS

First of all, I'd like to thank everyone at Bonnier
Books UK for supporting me throughout and for
running the ever-expanding UFH ship so smoothly.
Writing stories for the next generation of football fans
is both an honour and a pleasure. Thanks also to my
agent, Nick Walters, for helping to keep my dream
job going, year after year.

Next up, an extra big cheer for all the teachers,
booksellers and librarians who have championed these
books, and, of course, for the readers. The success
of this series is truly down to you.

Okay, onto friends and family. I wouldn't be writing
this series if it wasn't for my brother Tom. I owe him

so much and I'm very grateful for his belief in me as an author. I'm also very grateful to the rest of my family, especially Mel, Noah, Nico, and of course Mum and Dad. To my parents, I owe my biggest passions: football and books. They're a real inspiration for everything I do.

Pang, Will, Mills, Doug, Naomi, John, Charlie, Sam, Katy, Ben, Karen, Ana (and anyone else I forgot) – thanks for all the love and laughs, but sorry, no I won't be getting 'a real job' anytime soon!

And finally, I couldn't have done any of this without Iona's encouragement and understanding. Much love to you.

CHAPTER 1

AN ENGLAND HERO AGAIN!

18 November 2020, Wembley Stadium

When the England players emerged through the tunnel, everything was silent, except for the clatter of studs and the echoing words of the stadium announcer:

'...ENGLAND VERSUS ICELAND!!'

Phil Foden still found it strange walking out onto a football pitch without hearing the stirring sounds of a crowd all around him, even though it was nine months now since the start of the COVID-19 pandemic. It seemed especially weird at Wembley, where he had enjoyed so many cup final celebrations with his club, Manchester City.

Phil didn't need a party atmosphere to motivate him for this particular match, though! Although England's chances of UEFA Nations League glory were already over, he still had plenty to play for. He was starting only his second senior game for his country, and it felt like a second chance. After his debut in September, he had been sent home in disgrace for breaking team COVID-19 rules, but since then, he had worked hard to win his place back in Gareth Southgate's squad. Now, it was time for Phil to repay his manager's faith with a creative masterclass against Iceland.

Harry Kane, Jack Grealish and Phil Foden – what an entertaining England attack! With so much skill on show, there was sure to be goals. When he first got the ball, Phil glided past his opponent with two silky-smooth touches and a burst of speed. He was really in the mood to make things happen today. On the right, on the left, in the middle – Phil was popping up all over the pitch, always passing and moving, passing and moving, in that style his City manager Pep Guardiola loved.

Phil was on fire, but could he find that killer ball to break through the defence? In the twentieth minute, England won a free kick on the left, just outside the Iceland penalty area. Two players stood over it – one right-footed, one left-footed. The inswinger or the outswinger, which would it be? The outswinger! After a short run-up, Phil whipped a dangerous, left-foot cross into the six-yard box, where Declan Rice flicked the ball down into bottom corner with his shoulder. *1–0!*

Hurray, Phil had his first-ever England assist! As the players raced over to hug Declan, Kieran Trippier stopped to high-five the free-kick taker. 'Well done, mate, but I'm taking the next one, okay?!' he said with a smile.

Mason Mount soon added a second goal, and after that, Phil pushed forward, searching for a goal of his own. He was a regular scorer for City and for the England youth teams too, including two to help win the Under-17 World Cup final. But a first senior international strike here would be the perfect way to celebrate his return to Southgate's side...

Phil dribbled his way into the six-yard box, but he couldn't quite beat the keeper. *SAVED!*

Oooooooooohhhh!

Next, he sprinted into a pocket of space and fired a low shot from outside the area, but the keeper dived across and somehow tipped the ball just past the post. *SAVED!*

Arrrrggggghhhhh!

It was a real hands-on-head moment for Phil. How on earth had that not gone in? He was playing so well, but was he ever going to score?

Midway through the second half, Southgate started making substitutions:

Harry Winks on for... Mason,

Tammy Abraham on for... Harry,

Phil's old City academy teammate Jadon Sancho on for... Jack.

Phew, so Phil could stay on for now – and there was still time for him to score! With ten minutes to go, Jadon played a one-two with Bukayo Saka on the left wing and burst into the box. Jadon could have taken a shot himself, but instead he slipped a pass across to his friend Phil, who swept the ball first-time into the bottom corner. *3–0!*

Goooooooooooooooooooaaaaaaaaaaaaaaaaallllllllllllllll llllllllllll!!!!!!!!!!!!!!!!!!!!!

'Yessssssssss!' Phil roared, punching the air with both fists. He had done it; he had scored his first England goal! Then he turned around and pointed at the teammate who had helped make it happen. Three years on from winning the Under-17 World Cup together, the Young Lions were linking up again for the seniors.

'Thanks mate – you're the best!' he told Jadon as they hugged.

Phil was having too much fun to stop there. Just moments later, he got the ball in the middle and took a touch inside to create space for another shot. BANG! The ball skipped and swerved right into the bottom corner again. *4–0!*

Goooooooooooooooooooaaaaaaaaaaaaaaaaallllllllllllllll llllllllllll!!!!!!!!!!!!!!!!!!!!!

Unstoppable! With a big grin on his face, Phil jogged over to celebrate with Declan.

'Nice one, mate,' his teammate shouted as he threw his arms around him. 'You're on a hat-trick now!'

Sadly, Phil couldn't grab a third goal of the game, but he almost set up one up for Bukayo with a beautiful cross to the back post. Then, to finish off his man-of-the-match performance, Phil produced a moment of true football magic. As a high ball dropped towards him wide on the right touchline, he had the confidence and the quality to control it with an incredible *Cruyff Turn*. Wow, what a genius skill – if only there had been fans at Wembley to watch him!

At the final whistle, it ended 4–0 to England – job done, and especially for Phil. After a difficult few months, he was back to being a hero again. One assist, two goals, and too many classy touches to count; what a remarkable return to the national team! Thank goodness his manager had given him a second chance to shine.

'I'm really pleased for Foden, he's such an exciting player,' Southgate said after the game. 'He'll be fabulous for England for years.'

That was a big claim to make about a twenty-year-old, but Phil was no ordinary young footballer. It had been clear to everyone that the boy would become a superstar, ever since his first kicks in Stockport.

CHAPTER 2

THE FIRST KICKS OF RONNIE ROUNDHEAD

'Look at him go – he's almost crawling already!' Phil Foden Senior cried out joyfully as he watched his seven-month-old son shuffle and wriggle his way across the playmat.

His wife, Claire, however, wasn't quite so excited about that idea. 'Great, that's all we need,' she replied, rolling her eyes, 'another active little boy!'

The Fodens already had one energetic son, Callum, running around the house, and very soon, it seemed, they would have a second. Because despite still being months away from his first birthday, Phil Junior was determined to do everything his elder brother did: walk, then run, and then, best of all, play football!

Yes, like a lot of people in the area where they lived, the Fodens were a big football family. You could see the Stockport County stadium from their house in Edgeley, plus Manchester City's Main Road was only six miles away, and most importantly for Phil Senior, Manchester United's Old Trafford was less than ten miles away. He had been a talented footballer himself when he was younger, and he was eager to pass on his passion to his sons. Who knew? Perhaps one of them would one day fulfil his dream of becoming a professional in the Premier League! After watching lots of football matches together on TV, Callum was already an avid player and Manchester United supporter. Now, he just needed to persuade Phil Junior to join the club.

To his dad's delight, it didn't take long at all for the youngest Foden to become a football fan. He loved the little ball that his parents had attached to his pram, but after a while he got bored of just sitting there, tapping and kicking it; no, he wanted to be on his feet and moving around with it! And so by the age of just ten months, he was already up and walking.

'Mum, Dad – Ronnie's ready to play with me now!'
Callum cheered, holding an inflatable football above
his head in celebration.

Although his real name was Phil, just like his father,
everyone in the family called him 'Ronnie' instead. His
grandmother had come up with the nickname because
when he was born, his little head looked as round as
a football. 'He's a Ronnie Roundhead!' she announced
one day, and the name just stuck.

At first, Callum was the football master and Ronnie
was his young student, developing his skills in the
family living room, each and every day. However, it
didn't take long for those roles to change because it
turned out that Ronnie was an absolute natural. By
the age of two, not only could he kick and control the
ball brilliantly, but he could also dribble around with it
tight to his little left foot. Wow – how had he learned
to play like that at such a young age?! Callum tried his
best to tackle his baby brother, but to his frustration,
he was finding it harder and harder to stop him.

'Woah, Ronnie's really got something special!'
Phil Senior realised, watching him weave his way

past Callum as if he was just a practice cone. And he wasn't the only one who had spotted his son's exciting potential. 'That kid could play for England one day!' Ronnie's grandfather Walter declared on one occasion after they had spent hours together practising volleys in the garden.

It was a bold prediction to make about a three-year-old boy, but why not? As well as the talent, Ronnie also had the passion and desire. He was absolutely football mad already! All he ever wanted to do was practise his skills: dribbling, passing, shooting, heading, tackling. He wasn't interested in other games or toys like most young children. There was only one present that he really wanted for each and every birthday: a brand-new ball.

'Thanks Mum, thanks Dad! Can Callum and I go out and play with it now?'

CHAPTER 3

SCOUTED AT SCHOOL!

The exciting news spread like wildfire through the corridors of Bridge Hall Primary School, from Callum's Year 6 class all the way down to Phil in Year 1 – a Manchester City scout was coming!

At that time in 2005, City weren't as successful as their local rivals United, but still, they were a big Premier League club with famous footballers like David James, Danny Mills, Trevor Sinclair and Andy Cole in their squad. Plus, they also had lots of young players like Kasper Schmeichel, Nedum Onuoha, Joey Barton and Micah Richards, who had all come through the City academy and were now starring for the first team. Maybe one of the boys at Bridge Hall

Primary could be next!

When the momentous day arrived, every young player at the school was desperate to put on their best performance and impress the City scout. Terry John was his name and he had years of experience when it came to spotting the most promising young players in the Manchester area. In recent years, he had discovered two very talented footballers called Ravel Morrison and Marcus Rashford, but in the end, both had decided to join United instead.

So, would Terry John find any future City stars at Bridge Hall Primary? At first, that didn't look very likely. The scout watched the Year 6 training session, but unfortunately no-one really caught his eye, not even Callum. It was always worth having a look, just in case. John was ready to say goodbye and return home, but before he left the school that day, he made the very wise decision to ask the PE teacher if there were any other, younger kids that he thought he should see.

Mr Cartwright nodded his head immediately and with great enthusiasm – he knew just the boy. 'Phil

Foden. He's still only five years old, but wow! He's going to be a FANTASTIC footballer when he's older.'

Interesting! 'Why don't you bring him out here for a one-to-one training session?' the scout suggested.

Great idea! When Mr Cartwright walked into his Year 1 classroom and asked to have a word with him, Phil initially thought he was in trouble. Uh-oh, what had he done wrong? But no – instead of a telling-off, the teacher gave him an invitation.

'Phil, I'm sure you've heard that there's a City scout at our school today. Well, I've been telling him all about you, and he'd like you to come outside and show off your football skills,' Mr Cartwright explained. 'What do you think – are you up for that?'

A kickaround? With someone from Manchester City? Yeah, Phil was definitely up for that! He was too young to feel nervous about such an amazing opportunity. Instead, as he entered the playground and shook Mr John's hand, he couldn't wait to get started. He was going to have so much fun! This was a chance to play football, the thing he loved more than anything else, so what was there to worry about?

'Really? He's barely taller than the ball!' That was Terry John's first thought as Phil walked towards him with a big grin on his face, ready to play. But the scout's doubts soon disappeared once he saw the boy in action. Wow, what a natural!

Touch? *Tick!* He could already control the ball beautifully.

Passing? *Tick!* He had plenty of power in his little left foot, and accuracy too.

Dribbling? *Tick!* As he weaved his way through the cones, he moved with perfect balance.

He was a joy to watch, and there was more to come when Mr John organised a little match at the end. Even at the age of five, as he got the ball, Phil was lifting his head up and looking around him, checking for opponents trying to tackle him and also teammates in space. Incredible – he had the awareness of a professional player already!

With every clever pass and movement, John's excitement grew and grew. It was always a thrill to discover a new top young talent, but he had never ever seen a five-year-old footballer as good as Phil! He had found a future City star at Bridge Hall Primary, after all. Now, he just needed to sign him up fast, before United could get there first.

'Well done, kid – you've really got something special! Fancy coming down to the City academy?' John said to Phil at the end of the session, before handing him a card with the club badge on it, as well as his name and details. 'Give this to your parents when you get home and ask them to give me a call.'

'Thanks very much, I will!' Phil replied with a beaming smile. For the rest of the afternoon, he held the card tightly in his hand as if it was a winning lottery ticket, and refused to let go in case he lost it. Then, at the end of the school day, he rushed outside, waving it in the air. He was buzzing and bursting to share his astonishing news:

'Mum, guess what? City want to sign me!'

CHAPTER 4

SIZE VS SKILL

'Wow, that's brilliant, Ronnie – yes, we'll give the man a call tonight, I promise!'

Of course Phil Senior wished it had been Manchester United rather than City, but he hid his disappointment well. Never mind, the main thing was that his young son was about to begin playing at a Premier League academy. What an opportunity!

Once his dad had spoken to Mr John on the phone, Phil Junior was all set to get started at City. Hurray! Again, there were no nerves, only huge excitement. 'I can't wait for this!' he told his dad in the car on the way to Platt Lane. And from the moment he arrived at his very first training session, Phil fitted in

perfectly and felt right at home. He liked the coaches
and the coaches liked him too. It helped that he was
the perfect football pupil: already really talented, but
also eager to learn more. The coaches only ever had
to show Phil something once and that was it – he
worked hard until he mastered it.

'Yes, that's it, what a run – it's like watching Lionel
Messi!'

'Boys, did you see the way Phil turned there with
the ball? That's what we want you all to do!'

But while Phil really enjoyed the weekly training
sessions, they were never enough to satisfy him. No,
when it came to football, he was always hungry for
more – more shots, more skills, and more matches. He
was still too young to officially sign for City and play
proper games for the academy, so what else could he
do while he waited? On top of the training sessions,
the break-time battles at Bridge Hall Primary and the
after-school street football with his mates in Edgeley,
Phil also began playing for a local Stockport team
called Reddish Vulcans at the weekends.

When he signed for the Vulcans, he was only seven

years old but once the coaches saw what the kid could do with the ball, they moved him straight up to the next age group. Even there, however, Phil was still a level above everyone else. In his first match, he was at the centre of everything, gliding across the grass past opponent after opponent, as if it was the easiest thing in the world.

'Who's the new boy there with the left foot?' the parent of one of the other Vulcans players asked. 'Where's he come from?'

The manager, Joe Makin, just smiled and gave a one-word reply: 'Heaven.'

The kid could do it all – pass, dribble, cross, shoot – and when he got the ball, it almost always led to a goal. He was an absolute joy to watch, and for now, he was a Vulcans player.

'Right, we better make the most of this one-in-a-million opportunity,' Makin thought to himself.

While there was no doubt whatsoever that Phil had the skills to succeed as a footballer, there was still one thing that worried some people: his size. He was the smallest player on his team and usually the smallest player on the whole pitch, but he didn't let that bother him. He was used to it by now, after years of battling against his elder brother Callum and against friends who were bigger and more physical than him.

Besides, size wasn't everything in a sport like football. At this particular time, Barcelona were one of the best teams in the world and their star players Messi, Xavi and Andrés Iniesta were all considered small. But that never stopped them from shining!

Like those Barcelona superstars, Phil had other major strengths that were far more important than height: determination, technique and intelligence. 'You use your brain well enough anyway. You don't need size and you don't need to do anything differently.' That's what one of the City coaches had told him once and he had never forgotten it. So if a defender tried to muscle him off the ball, Phil used his quick feet to escape and then used his awareness and vision to pick out a perfect pass to a teammate…

Goooooooooooooooooooaaaaaaaaaaaaaaaalllllllllllllll llllllllllll!!!!!!!!!!!!!!!!!!!

With their little wizard creating magic, the Vulcans

became a formidable football team. They won match after match, and trophy after trophy, including the 2008 North West Junior Champions League.

Phil loved his two seasons as a Vulcan, but eventually his time at the club came to an end. Why? Because as soon as he turned nine, he could sign his first contract with Manchester City! It was a moment that he had been waiting years for, as City had too. What a relief! At last, Phil was officially a City player and they no longer needed to worry about losing him to their rivals, United.

'Right, are you ready to become City's next superstar?' his academy coaches asked.

'Of course, can't wait!' Phil said with a smile.

CHAPTER 5

FOOTBALL AND FISHING WITH DAD

As he worked his way up through the City academy, Phil was fortunate to have a big support network of people around him: coaches, teammates, friends, and most importantly of all, family. What would he do without them?

There was his big brother, Callum, who was always up for a laugh and a kickaround.

There was his kind mum, Claire, who looked after him so well and sometimes took him to watch the City first team play at the City of Manchester Stadium.

And there was his dad, Phil Sr, who drove him to every training session and never missed a single match he played. Regardless of the weather or the distance he had to travel, he was there on the sidelines at all times, watching and cheering on his son:

'Well done, Ronnie – what a strike that was!'

Despite his passion for the game, Phil Sr tried not to be one of those pushy parents that he often saw shouting at their kids during academy matches. He wanted his son to enjoy his football and follow his own path, but if Phil Jr ever asked for any assistance, he was always there and happy to help.

'Dad, can we go and work on my long passes?' Phil Jr asked one day, and so they drove to an empty car park where they had lots of extra space.

'Dad, I want to work on my first touch,' Phil Jr said one day, and so they snuck onto a bowling green at night and sent the ball zipping across the smooth surface to each other.

As they practised together, Phil Sr was careful not to overwhelm his son with lots of coaching tips, but there was one piece of advice that he gave again and again:

'Get in the pockets!'

It was a phrase that Phil Jr had heard his dad say

so many times that it was imprinted on his brain as if with a permanent marker. But what did it mean? The 'pockets' were the spaces on the pitch in between the opposition midfield and defence, where an attacking playmaker like Phil could be particularly dangerous. Should a midfielder drop back to mark him, or should a defender move forward? Either way, it shifted the shape of the team and caused lots of uncertainty. If Phil could find the pockets and receive the ball there, then he would have the time to turn and create moments of magic for the City Under-9s…

Goooooooooooooooooooooaaaaaaaaaaaaaaaalllllllllllll llllllllllll!!!!!!!!!!!!!!!!!!

'Thanks Dad!'

During those early years at the City academy, the two Phils spent a lot of time together, especially as football wasn't the only passion that they shared.

Their love for fishing had all started one summer, when Phil Jr was seven years old. His dad had found an old fishing rod that belonged to his own father and he suggested that they should go and try it out at a local lake. Sure, why not?! With the football season over, Phil Jr was looking for something else to do. Sitting by the water waiting for fish to take the bait didn't sound very exciting, but he was happy to give it a go. And to his great surprise, he really enjoyed it!

Phil knew that his passion for football would never fade, but he found that it was nice to focus on a different activity for a bit. In many ways, fishing was the exact opposite of football. Instead of noisy crowds and fast-paced action, it was all about quiet, nature and patience. A lot of the time, it was just a father and his son sat chatting and relaxing in the sunshine, while whole hours passed by without them catching a single fish!

'Dad, is this it?' Phil moaned on that first morning.

But the more he learned about fishing, the more he loved it. Like football, there were lots of tactics to think about. Where would the biggest fish be? How deep would they be swimming, and so how long should their lines be? What would be the best bait to use to catch them?

And when Phil did finally feel the pull of a fish on the rod, wow, what a buzz!

'Dad, Dad, come quick – I think I've caught something!'

'Right, it's time to reel it in, Ronnie!'

Phil would never forget his first catch, and the proud feeling as he held it in his hands while his dad took a photo. Okay, it may not have been a very big fish, and nothing could ever compare to scoring a great goal, but still, it made him want to carry on fishing.

'Dad, can we do this again next weekend?' Phil asked on the drive home.

'Of course, son. That was just the beginning – there are plenty more fish in the lakes round here, and bigger ones too!'

'Thanks Dad!'

In the years to come, fishing would be a very important way for Phil to chill out and forget about football for a while, especially as things got more and more serious at Manchester City.

CHAPTER 6

PHIL,
THE CITY FAN

For 363 days of each year, the two Phils were best of
friends, in fishing and in football. For the other two,
however, they were bitter enemies. Why? Because of
the big Manchester derby!

The football rivalry split the family straight down
the middle:

Phil Sr and Callum supported United,

And Phil Jr and Claire supported City.

Oooooooooohhhh, who would be the winners and
who would be the losers? Would Manchester be red
or blue? Let the battle and arguments begin!

For years, United had dominated the derby, but
finally, times were changing. In 2008, the year before

Phil signed his first youth contract with City, the club had been bought by the Abu Dhabi United Group, making them the new richest club in the Premier League. Suddenly, City had the money to compete with United and bring in superstar after superstar:

Robinho,

Vincent Kompany,

Carlos Tevez,

Kolo Touré,

Yaya Touré,

Mario Balotelli,

And Phil's personal favourite, David Silva.

Thanks to their major new signings, City were moving higher and higher up the Premier League table: tenth place in 2009, then fifth in 2010, then third in 2011.

'This is going to be our year!' Phil Jr declared with confidence at the start of the 2011–12 season. 'We're going to win the league!'

Ever since his very first training session at the academy, little Phil had been a massive Manchester City supporter. In 2007, he had even walked out onto the pitch as a mascot for a match against Sunderland, holding hands with winger Martin Petrov.

'One day, I'll be out here playing!' he had told himself as he looked up at the loud crowd above.

For now though, Phil was a fan in the stands at almost every City home game, and he had good reason to feel so confident about the 2011–12 season. Over the summer of 2011, the club had added three more superstars to their excellent squad: Gaël Clichy and Samir Nasri from Arsenal, and most exciting of all, Argentinian striker Sergio Agüero from Atlético Madrid. On the opening day of the season, City thrashed Swansea City 4–0, with Agüero scoring twice.

'Oh man, I can't wait for the next Manchester derby!' Phil Jr teased his dad and brother. Away at Old Trafford, 23 October – only two months to wait!

When Derby Day finally arrived, City sat top of the table with twenty-two points, two points ahead of second-placed United. Wow, it was all set to be a really important match! Most fans were expecting a tight, tense battle, but in the end, it turned out to be a very one-sided game.

Balotelli fired the ball into the bottom corner. *1–0!*

Balotelli tapped in at the back post. *2–0!*

Agüero slid in to score. *3–0!*

Joleon Lescott's cross hit Edin Džeko on the knee and went in. *4–1!*

Silva slotted the ball through David de Gea's legs. *5–1!*

In the final minute, Džeko raced forward to add yet another goal. *6–1!*

What a thrashing! 6–1! At home in Edgeley, the United half of the Foden family sat there in stunned silence, while the City half danced around the living room in delight. At last, Manchester was blue!

'Yeah, this is definitely going to be our year,' Phil thought to himself.

Or was it??? After disappointing away defeats to Sunderland, Everton and Swansea, City slipped back down to second place, with only eight games to go. When they then lost to Arsenal, Phil feared their title hopes were over – but no, City bounced back brilliantly.

4–0 vs West Brom,
6–1 vs Norwich City,
2–0 vs Wolves,
And 1–0 vs United.

Yes, City had done the Manchester derby double, and even more excitingly, if they could just win their last two matches of the season, they would be crowned Premier League Champions!

'Come on, we can do this!' Phil cheered in the crowd, urging his City heroes on.

1) Newcastle away

With his nerves jangling, Phil could hardly bear to watch the match on TV, especially when it was still 0–0 after seventy minutes. If they didn't score soon, United would overtake them again at the top! In the end, however, City managed to win 2–0, thanks to two late goals from Yaya Touré. Phew! They only needed one more victory now...

2) QPR at home

Phil's heart was already pounding in his chest as he took his seat behind the goal in the North Stand for the biggest game of his life. Kick-off was still half an hour away; what would he feel like once the match actually started?

'Come on, City!'

Earlier in the season, they had beaten QPR 3–2 away, but this game would be different. Both teams were under huge pressure to win: QPR to avoid relegation, and City to lift the league title. But only one of them would succeed…

'COME ON, CITY!'

Just before half-time, Pablo Zabaleta scored to give them the lead. *1–0!*

'Yessssssssss!' Phil cheered along with the other 45,000 City supporters. So far so good – they were almost Premier League Champions now!

Early in the second half, however, City lost their focus and QPR came back fighting.

First, Djibril Cissé hit a powerful shot past Joe Hart. *1–1!*

Then Jamie Mackie put them ahead with a diving header. *2–1!*

'Noooooooo!' Phil groaned along with the other

45,000 supporters. Now their rivals United were going to win the league instead! Unless…

'COME ON, CITY!'

With time running out, Silva curled a corner into the box and Džeko headed home. *2–2!*

City were back in the game, but they still needed one more goal, and there were only two minutes to go…

It was now or never as Agüero launched City's last attack. He played a pass through to Balotelli, who held the ball up and then passed it back as Agüero burst into the box…

In the North Stand behind the goal, Phil leapt to his feet in anticipation. He couldn't, could he?

Yes, he could! A QPR defender tried to tackle Agüero but he stayed on his feet and smashed a shot past the keeper. *3–2!*

'AGUERRRRRRRRRO!' screamed commentator Martin Tyler on TV.

Meanwhile there in the stadium, Phil went absolutely wild along with the other 45,000 City supporters. 'YESSSSSSSSSSS!' They had done it; they had won the Premier League title for the first time!

When the final whistle blew, the fans stormed onto the pitch to celebrate and Phil was right there in the middle of all the madness. Unbelievable scenes at the Etihad Stadium! It was an afternoon that he would never, ever forget. Playing for the City first team had always been his dream, but now Phil was more determined than ever to achieve it.

CHAPTER 7

PHIL, THE FUTURE CITY SUPERSTAR

Winning that first Premier League title was only the start for Manchester City. Their ambition was to keep building and building until they could become one of the biggest and most successful clubs in the whole world.

For the present, City's plan was to sign lots of experienced internationals, like Fernandinho from Brazil and Jesús Navas from Spain. That was clearly working well because the team would win the League and Cup double in 2014. However, if they wanted to maintain their position at the top for many years to come, they needed to think about the future as well as the present.

Although they were very rich, the City owners didn't want to keep buying players from other clubs forever; they also wanted to start developing superstars of their own. And so for the future, they spent £50 million on a brand-new football complex, where all of their teams could train together: male, female, first team and academy.

Woah! As Phil arrived at The City Football Academy when it first opened in December 2014, he felt like he had just entered football heaven. Not only were the facilities incredible, but from now on, he would also be training right next to his heroes. There was Agüero practising his shooting against Hart, and there was his idol Silva doing a passing drill with Yaya Touré and Nasri!

It was an amazing opportunity for the young players to watch and learn up close, and a clever way to inspire them too. Not that Phil really needed any extra motivation; he was already so determined to become a City legend and their next great homegrown hero.

With so many expensive superstars in front of him, Phil knew that his journey to the first team wasn't

going to be easy, but he believed in himself and so did
his academy coaches. Ever since his early days in the
Under-9s, he had stood out as a future City superstar.
In game after game, he got the ball and glided
gracefully past his opponents, even those who were
two years older and much bigger and stronger than
him. With his vision and skill, there was usually only
one way the story ended:

*Goooooooooooooooooooooaaaaaaaaaaaaaaaalllllllllllllll
lllllllllllll!!!!!!!!!!!!!!!!!!!*

'Wow, he's unbelievable! How on earth did he do
that and make it look so easy?'

By the time Phil turned fourteen, everyone at the
club agreed that the tiny kid from Stockport had a
rare natural talent, which needed to be protected
and handled with care. So, as he progressed through
the youth teams, Jason Wilcox and Scott Sellars tried
not to over-coach him. Instead, they concentrated
on helping him to make the most of the outstanding
ability he already had.

'That's it – receive the ball on the run and GO!'

'Keep getting into those gaps – that way, when the

ball comes, you'll be able to turn and escape before the big defenders come clattering in!'

It wasn't just Phil's football skills that impressed his coaches, though; it was also his attitude. He was a model student, eager to listen and eager to learn. Yes, he was blessed with natural football talent, but he knew that wasn't enough on its own. With so much competition for places at the City academy, Phil also had to work hard and stay humble and dedicated. So he made sure that he was always one of the earliest to arrive at training, and also one of the last to leave. Every day, he battled to be the best at everything: passing, dribbling, shooting, sprinting…

'Okay, let's stop together,' Phil agreed with his speedy new teammate Jadon Sancho, once they were the last players left running in the beep test.

Phil just had so much enthusiasm for the game, and also for his club. His love of City was so strong that he was still asking to be a ball boy at the Etihad Stadium even when he was playing for the Under-18s!

'I think you might be a bit old for that now,' Wilcox had to tell him in the end. 'Besides, you're on your way to bigger and better things, lad!'

Phil's first-team dream was getting closer and closer. In May 2016, he was part of the squad that lifted the Under-18s Premier League trophy, and when many of the senior players then moved up to the Under-23s, Phil was ready to step up and become a regular starter. City's new line-up for 2016–17 featured Jadon on one wing, Luke Bolton on the other, Joe Hardy or Lorenzo González as the central striker, and Phil pulling the strings as the midfield playmaker – what an amazing attack!

The City Under-18s started the new season on fire, with Jadon grabbing goals against West Brom and Everton, and then Phil scoring two in a 7–0 thrashing of Liverpool. Soon, it was time for their biggest game of the year – the Manchester derby against United! With the pressure on, it was City's young stars who shone brightest. Jadon set up the first goal for Luke Bolton and then in the second half, Phil cut inside off the left wing and found the pocket of space he needed to make it 2–0.

Goooooooooooooooooooooaaaaaaaaaaaaaaaaalllllllllllllll

IIIIIIIIIIIIII!!!!!!!!!!!!!!!!!!!!!!!

'Mate, we did it – Manchester is blue!' Jadon
cheered as City's future superstars celebrated the
derby win together. It was all set to be a breakthrough
year for them both.

CHAPTER 8

PEP'S KIND OF PLAYER

After many years of trying, in July 2016, Manchester City finally got the manager they really wanted – Pep Guardiola! The Spaniard was a tactical genius, most famous for transforming Barcelona into the best team in the world by encouraging them to play free-flowing, passing football. As a result, his side had won three league titles and two Champions League trophies in just four seasons. So, could he do the same at City? That was the hope!

Guardiola's arrival at the club was greeted with great excitement, by the fans and also by the players. At last, this was the manager who was going to take the team to the next level and help them win the

Champions League! After all, he had done it before at Barcelona, where he had worked with the likes of Messi, Xavi, Iniesta, Dani Alves, Thierry Henry... the list of superstars went on and on.

However, as well as anticipation, there was also a slight sense of fear amongst the City first-team squad. Because what if Pep didn't like them? What if they weren't his kind of players? Guardiola wanted his team to play 'tiki-taka' football:

Pass and move, pass and move, pass and move, pass and move... *GOAL!*

It was a style of play that suited some of the City players perfectly, especially creative midfielders like David Silva and Kevin De Bruyne. Oh, and also a certain sixteen-year-old who coaches were already calling 'The Stockport Iniesta'...

'You have to see this one kid at the academy,' the director of football, Txiki Begiristain, told Pep during preseason, on one of his first days at City. 'He's definitely your kind of player!'

'Okay, what's his name?'

'Phil Foden.'

'Well, invite him to come and train with the first team for a day.'

When his Under-18s manager, Lee Carsley, told him the news, Phil couldn't believe it. Practising next to the heroes he'd grown up watching was already awesome, but sharing the same pitch as David Silva and Agüero... wow, that was going to be AMAZING!

'Come on, let's show them what we can do!' Phil told Jadon and Brahim Díaz, who had also been invited to train with the first team.

Once the training session started, however, Phil was too shy to say much to his new superstar teammates. Instead, he let his football skills do the talking, and tried to listen and learn as much as possible. He was doing passing drills with David Silva, while being coached by Pep Guardiola – and what an unbelievable opportunity it was! Phil was determined to make the most of it.

And he did. While Jadon and Brahim were both lively and showed flashes of their potential, it was the little midfield playmaker who really stood out for Pep. 'Wow, did you see that kid in the centre of the field?' he asked his coaches. The City manager was so impressed that he invited Phil back for a second day of training.

'You were right, Txiki,' Pep told his Director of Football afterwards. 'This player is really good!'

Phil returned to the Under-18s feeling proud and inspired. He had challenged himself against world-class internationals and he hadn't looked out of place at all. In fact, he looked and felt like he belonged there. So, if he kept working hard and doing what he was doing, he was confident that he would get more first-team chances in the future. Even he, however, was surprised at how soon his next opportunity arrived.

In the Champions League, City had managed to qualify for the Round of 16 with one match to spare. So for their final home game against Celtic, Pep decided to make changes and give his young players a chance.

In defence: teenagers Tosin Adarabioyo and Pablo Maffeo.

In attack: Kelechi Iheanacho.

And on the subs bench: goalkeeper Angus Gunn, left-back Angeliño, and youngest of all of City's academy stars... midfield magician Phil Foden!

The call-up had been a complete surprise for Phil because he wasn't even training with the first team at the time. One day, he was playing for the Under-18s and the next, he got a phone call saying, 'You're going to be on the bench in the Champions League.' Really?! It sounded unbelievable, but no, it was actually happening. At the age of only sixteen, Phil had been included in his first senior matchday squad, and he even had his own shirt number now: Number 80!

'Congratulations, Ronnie!' his proud parents cried, jumping for joy when they heard the incredible news. If Pep brought him on, their son would become City's youngest-ever Champions League player. What an achievement that would be!

Phil watched on from the bench with butterflies in his stomach and restless legs as Kelechi gave City the lead and then Celtic equalised. It remained 1–1 throughout the second half, but unfortunately his potential record-breaking moment never appeared.

Oh well – it had still been a great experience to warm up with the senior players in front of thousands of fans at the Etihad. Phil would never forget the moment when he had first walked out onto the pitch and heard the fans clapping and cheering for their new homegrown hero. Wow, what a feeling!

Phil returned to the Under-18s with extra fire in his belly and switched his focus to his next goal: winning the FA Youth Cup. For two years in a row, City had reached the final before losing to rivals Chelsea. So, could they go all the way and lift the trophy at last, with Phil, Jadon and Brahim all in the same team?

City cruised through the early rounds, squeezed past Aston Villa in the quarters and then thrashed Stoke City in the semis to set up a final against... yes, Chelsea again! Phil and his teammates were determined that this third time would be different.

The first leg of the final was at home at the Academy Stadium. While City really wanted to win, they knew they couldn't afford to lose, but by half-time, that's exactly what they were doing. Uh-oh, could their young stars step up and save the day?

Yes! After the break, City battled their way back
into the game. Jadon teamed up with Tyreke Wilson
to win the ball on the left wing and pass it quickly
across to Phil, who had finally found a pocket of space
behind the Chelsea midfield...

DANGER ALERT! As Phil turned and dribbled
forward, there was nothing the defenders could do to
stop him. From just inside the box, he calmly curled a
shot into the bottom corner. *1–1!*

*Gooooooooooooooooooooaaaaaaaaaaaaaaaaalllllllllllllll
llllllllllll!!!!!!!!!!!!!!!!!!!!!!*

Game on! Phil punched the air in celebration
down on the pitch, and meanwhile, the City manager
was doing the same thing up in the boardroom. Yes,
Guardiola was watching, and he was very excited by
what he saw. This kid was very, very special!

A week later, though, City lost the second leg 5–1
at Stamford Bridge and Chelsea won the FA Youth
Cup yet again. Phil was disappointed, of course, but
he tried to focus on the positives. He was learning fast
and becoming a better player with every experience,

win or lose. And hopefully, he wouldn't have to wait too long for a second taste of first-team life. But whether it came next week or next year, Phil knew that his time would come eventually at City. Why? Because he was Pep's kind of player.

CHAPTER 9

YOUNG LIONS
PART I

By now, it was clear to everyone that Phil was a future
superstar, and not just for Manchester City, but for
England too. So, after eight excellent performances
for the Under-16s, including two goals against Brazil,
Steve Cooper decided to call him up to the Under-17s
squad.

The year 2017 was looking like it could be a very
busy one for the England Under-17s, with a European
Championships in May, followed by a World Cup in
October. Their aim was to win both competitions, and
Cooper was building the best possible team to do so.
He already had Marc Guéhi and Jonathan Panzo in
defence, George McEachran in central midfield, Jadon

and Callum Hudson-Odoi on the wings, and Rhian Brewster up front, but he believed that Phil was the missing piece of the puzzle.

It certainly looked that way when Phil scored on his debut against Belgium, and there was even better to come in the Euro qualifiers against Romania. In only the second minute of the match, Phil got the ball near the halfway line, turned beautifully and dribbled forward with skill and balance, past one defender, then another, then another... It was a magical run, but he made it look so easy, and as he entered the box, he curled a left-foot shot past the keeper. *1–0!*

Goooooooooooooooooooooaaaaaaaaaaaaaaaalllllllllllllll lllllllllll!!!!!!!!!!!!!!!!!!!!

Phil threw his arms out wide and smiled as his teammates raced over to celebrate with him. Ten minutes later, he scored again, this time a clever free kick into the bottom corner. Wow, what a special player!

'Euros, here we come!' Phil roared with passion. He couldn't wait to represent his country at the tournament in Croatia. It was going to be a great opportunity to test himself against the top young players from all over Europe, and hopefully, to help his team to bring home the trophy.

That didn't look very likely, at first, against Norway in their first game of the tournament. After just seven minutes, they were 1–0 down, but they had the quality and belief to turn things around.

Jadon dribbled into the box and crossed the ball to Rhian. *1–1!*

Callum set up Rhian to score his second. *2–1!*

And in the final moments of the match, Phil glided into the penalty area and calmly chipped the ball over the keeper. *3–1!*

Gooooooooooooooooooooaaaaaaaaaaaaaaaaaalllllllllllllll llllllllllll!!!!!!!!!!!!!!!!!!!

Phil and his teammates celebrated with hugs and high-fives – job done, match won! Onto the next one...

After that early shock against Norway, England had upped their game and they cruised past Ukraine and the Netherlands into the quarter-finals. There, they faced a tough Ireland team who defended well, but a moment of magic from Jadon was enough to send England through.

'Come onnnnn, we're going all the way!' the Young Lions cheered together.

In the semi-finals, Turkey made life very difficult for England, but in the end, the team with the best attackers won.

Jadon slid a pass through to Callum, who curled a shot into the top corner. *1–0!*

Then with half-time approaching, Phil received the ball just outside the Turkey penalty area and turned in a flash. What next? He was surrounded by six opponents, but somehow he still had the composure and awareness to spot Jadon on the run and play the perfect, defence-splitting pass to find him. *2–0!*

'Yesssssssssss!' Phil yelled as he jumped on Jadon's back. City's young stars were on fire for England, and they were through to the Euro final! Now, if they could just beat Spain, they would be the champions, and the trophy would be theirs.

The pressure was on, but the Young Lions began the final confidently, like it was any other game. In the eighteenth minute, Jadon passed the ball to Callum, who cut inside off the left wing and curled the ball into the top corner once again. *1–0 to England!*

Phil sprinted over to join his teammates as they slid towards the corner flag on their knees. What a start!

Spain, however, were too good to go down without a fight. They bounced back before half-time, as Mateu Morey finished off a flowing team move. *1–1!*

It was all to play for in the second half, but which team would win it? And which young star could create a moment of match-winning magic?

In the fifty-seventh minute, Spain cleared an England corner-kick, but only as far as Phil on the edge of the area. This was it; the chance he'd been waiting for. After a calm touch to control the ball, he looked up at the target. Should he try to fire a shot into the top corner? No, he decided to surprise the keeper instead, by sending a low rocket fizzing through the crowded box and into the bottom corner. *2–1 to England!*

Goooooooooooooooooooaaaaaaaaaaaaaaaalllllllllllllll llllllllllllll!!!!!!!!!!!!!!!!!!!!!

'Get in!' Phil yelled as he punched the air with both
fists. When his team needed something special, he had
delivered it like a real big-game player. England's hero
was soon at the centre of a big, sweaty squad hug.

'Yesssss, you legend!'

'Mate, that was magic!'

It looked like Phil's goal would surely be the
winner, but no – in the last seconds of the final, Spain
bounced back again. A header from Nacho Díaz
somehow squeezed past the keeper and defenders on
the goal-line. *2–2!*

Nooooooooooo! It was a devastating blow for
England because not only was the final now going to
penalties, but Cooper had just subbed off Jadon and
Phil, two of his penalty takers! Instead of stepping up,
they had to watch from the sidelines as Rhian and
then Joel Latibeaudiere missed their spot-kicks. Spain,
not England, were the new Under-17 Champions of
Europe.

NOOOOOOOOO!

Phil really hated losing any football match, so losing
a massive Euros final – and less than a month after

losing the FA Youth Cup Final with City – was the worst feeling in the world, like a painful punch in the gut. Once the first wave of disappointment faded, however, he was able to find the positives. With two great goals and an amazing assist, he had proved himself as one of England's most promising young players. Plus, this was only the beginning of Phil's big breakthrough year; he still had lots more to achieve, for both club and country.

CHAPTER 10

AN IMPRESSIVE PRESEASON

For Phil, everything was happening so fast that there wasn't time to feel too downhearted. Just twelve days after England's defeat in the Under-17 Euros final, the Manchester City chairman, Khaldoon Al Mubarak, made an announcement about City's stars of the future:

'What makes it special this year especially is that we have three or four players we genuinely believe have a very good chance of making it to the first team. You look at Sancho, you look at Phil Foden, you look at Brahim Díaz... these are players that are extremely talented.'

'Phil Foden – that's me!' Although he already knew

that Pep liked him and that he was progressing well at the academy, it was still a very proud moment to hear the City chairman pick him out as one of the club's stand-out youngsters.

But what did it really mean? Well, on top of lots more training with the first team, Phil, Jadon and Brahim were also asked to help launch the club's new home kit, and best of all, they were named in City's squad for their preseason tour to... the USA!

Outwardly, Phil tried to play it cool, but on the inside, his brain was screaming, 'Yessss, I've always wanted to go to Los Angeles!'

By the time they set off, City's three young stars had become two because Jadon had decided to leave and join Borussia Dortmund, but that didn't stop Phil from feeling excited about their first trip away with the first team. Together with Brahim, he was living his football dream!

Once they arrived, the players had a few days of training to get used to the heat and humidity, before it was time for the 2017 International Champions Cup to begin. In pre-season, some clubs liked to start slowly with slightly easier matches, but not City. No, they weren't messing around. To prepare for the new season, they were taking on three of the best teams in the world:

Real Madrid,

Tottenham,

And Manchester United!

For the derby match, Guardiola decided to go with a mix of youth and experience in his starting line-up. So he picked Tosin to play alongside Vincent in central defence, and Phil to play the David Silva role next to Yaya and Kevin in midfield!

It was a big responsibility for the little seventeen-year-old, especially in front of 67,000 fans, but Phil showed no fear, only excitement. This was his chance to impress the manager ahead of the new season, and he was determined to take it. He couldn't wait to test himself against Paul Pogba and Ander Herrera, and show that he belonged on the biggest stage.

Out on the pitch, the rituals of handshakes and team photos seemed to go on forever, but finally it was time to play football. 'Right, I'm ready for this,' Phil told himself as he practised one last leap before kick-off.

In the twelfth minute, he received the ball with his back to goal midway through the Manchester United half. As he looked over his shoulder, Phil spotted Herrera charging towards him, but with two clever, quick touches, he spun away into space and passed it through to Sergio.

'Hurraaaaaaaaay!' cheered the City supporters. What class, what composure!

'An impressive start from the Stockport lad,' the club posted on social media.

And as the game went on, Phil's confidence grew and grew. He was everywhere, battling for the ball, calling for the ball, and then passing and moving, passing and moving, just like he had learned from his manager.

Just before half-time, Phil played a one-two with Yaya, and this time, Phil decided to dribble forward himself. When he reached the edge of the United box, he hit a powerful shot that was heading for the top corner, until David De Gea dived across to tip it past the post.

'Unlucky, great effort!' called Phil's captain, Vincent, clapping and cheering behind him.

With sweat streaming down his face, Phil kept on running and creating chances, but unfortunately, he couldn't quite find that killer final pass or shot to win the game for City. Instead, it was United who won the derby 2–0.

Phil didn't feel too disappointed, though. In fact, he had loved every minute of it. The game had been a great experience for him, and with his magnificent display, he had certainly achieved his aim of impressing his manager.

'It's a long time since I saw something like this,' Guardiola said of him at the post-match press conference. 'His performance was another level.'

Phil kept his starting spot as City thrashed Real Madrid 4–1, but for the 3–0 win over Tottenham, David returned in the main playmaker role.

So, what next for Phil – first-team football? When the 2017–18 Premier League season started, Pep named him as a substitute for three out of City's first four matches. Sadly, however, Phil didn't get the chance to come on and make his debut, and once all the senior stars returned, he dropped out of the matchday squad and back down to the Under-23s.

Despite his successful preseason, Phil was still on the fringes of the City first team for now, but he was happy to be patient because he could clearly see the path ahead of him. If he kept working hard and playing well for the youth teams, Guardiola would be watching. Every match was a chance to impress the City manager, and the Under-17 World Cup in India was now just weeks away.

CHAPTER 11

YOUNG LIONS PART II

When it came to football, Phil was happy to play anytime, anywhere – in the changing room, in the showers, even in a hotel corridor. While the rest of his England Under-17 teammates relaxed in their rooms after training, Phil was there in his socks, kicking his mini football against the wall.

'Mate, could you please stop for just a few minutes?' goalkeeper Curtis Anderson called out wearily from behind the door. 'I'm trying to sleep in here!'

'Sorry, didn't mean to disturb you... Sure you don't fancy a kickaround?'

Corridor football was fun, but Phil couldn't wait

for the main event to get started. The 2017 FIFA Under-17 World Cup in India – what a brilliant tournament it was going to be! The Young Lions were one of the favourites to lift the trophy, and after losing to Spain in the Euros final in May, they were even more determined to go all the way this time. If they succeeded, they would become the first England team ever to win the Under-17 World Cup!

Their manager, Steve Cooper, had brought a few new faces into the squad, but mostly it was the same band of brothers from the Euros: Marc and Jonathan in defence, George McEachran in central midfield, and then that fantastic front four: Callum, Jadon, Rhian and Phil.

What a dream team! With all their tricks, flicks and clever one-twos, they were so, so difficult to stop. Callum and Jadon grabbed the goals in England's first game, against Chile, while Rhian scored a great free kick to give England the lead against Mexico. Then just after half-time, Jadon laid the ball across to Phil, who curled a first-time shot past the keeper from the edge of the box. *2–0!*

*Gooooooooooooooooooooaaaaaaaaaaaaaaaaalllllllllllllll
lllllllllllll!!!!!!!!!!!!!!!!!!!!!!*

As he raced over to the corner flag, Phil leapt up
and punched the air with passion. He had scored
his first World Cup goal! He loved being part of this
England team so much.

'Well done, all that practising in the hotel was
worth it!' joked Phil's best friend and roommate,
George.

With two wins out of two, the Young Lions were
through to the Round of 16. That was the good news;
the bad news was that Jadon wouldn't be joining them
there. Instead, he had to go back to his new German
club, Borussia Dortmund.

'Good luck!' he told his teammates. 'Go win it
without me!'

With Angel Gomes coming in, England's attack still
looked strong, but they really struggled without Jadon
against Japan. The match finished 0–0, but fortunately,
they won the penalty shoot-out. Phew!

'Come on, we're way better than that!' Phil told
his teammates after the match. He wasn't usually

much of a talker in the dressing room, but with Jadon gone, England needed someone else to step up and lead the way. Phil was ready to take on that extra responsibility.

In the quarter-finals against the USA, he helped the Young Lions get back to being unstoppable again. In the tenth minute, he weaved his way up the right wing with great skill and balance, before delivering a dangerous cross into the six-yard box. The keeper managed to punch the ball away, but only as far as Rhian. *1–0!*

'Yesssssssss!' Phil yelled, racing over to celebrate with his teammates. After that, it was all England, and Rhian finished with a hat-trick. They were through to the semi-finals!

The Young Lions were going to need to be at their very best, however, because their next opponents would be Brazil. Both teams were still unbeaten at the tournament, but only one could win and make it through to the World Cup Final...

In front of 63,000 fans in Kolkata, England started strongly. From wide on the left, Callum crossed the

ball in to Rhian, who scored at the second attempt.
1–0!

England's lead, however, didn't last long. Wesley
equalised for Brazil and Brenner almost added a
second goal shortly afterwards.

'Calm down and focus!' Cooper shouted from the
sidelines. What the England manager needed was
someone to step forward and create a moment of
magic for his team. Who could that be?

As Phil received the ball on the right, he could see
his teammate, Steven Sessegnon, sprinting forward on
the overlap. Great! He slowed his dribbling down and
waited until the perfect moment to play the pass to
Steven, who fired the ball first-time across the six-yard
box for Rhian to score. *2–1!*

'Yesssssssssss!' Phil screamed up at the sky as he
joined the wild England celebrations.

And his best semi-final moment was still to come.
Even four Brazilian players couldn't stop Phil as he
glided forward with the ball, from the halfway line all
the way to the penalty area. It was a remarkable run,
and at the end of it, Phil had the awareness to slide a

pass through to Emile Smith Rowe, who crossed it for Rhian to complete another hat-trick. *3–1!*

'YESSSSSSSSS!'

Game over – England were through to the World Cup Final! Phil's midfield masterclass was complete, and so Cooper took him off with five minutes to go. On the bench, Phil waited impatiently for the final whistle to blow and then threw his arms around his manager. They had done it – they had beaten Brazil! The Young Lions were now just one game away from lifting the trophy, and who were they playing in the final? Their old Euros enemies, Spain!

England were aiming for sweet revenge, but at half-time in Kolkata, they found themselves 2–1 down and heading towards another disappointing final defeat. No, no, no – Phil wasn't going to let that happen. Of course they could come back! He was determined to turn things around for his team. He was a big-game player and this was the biggest game of his life. It was time to stay calm and lead the Young Lions to victory.

From the moment the second half started, Phil showed the world that he was the best player on the pitch. He was at the centre of everything for England.

In the fifty-eighth minute, he got the ball in a pocket of space on the right and threaded another perfect pass through to Steven, who crossed it to Morgan. *2–2!*

Ten minutes later, Callum raced up the left wing and crossed to Phil, who coolly lifted the ball over the diving keeper. *3–2!*

Goooooooooooooooooooooaaaaaaaaaaaaaaaalllllllllllllll llllllllllll!!!!!!!!!!!!!!!!!!!!

The comeback was complete; England were now winning! As he ran over to the corner flag, Phil threw his head back and his arms out wide. It was a feeling that he would never forget.

The Young Lions weren't done yet, though. Marc reacted quickest in a goalmouth scramble. *4–2!*

And in the final seconds, Phil raced onto Callum's through-ball and slid a shot under the keeper. *5–2!*

Goooooooooooooooooooooaaaaaaaaaaaaaaaalllllllllllllll llllllllllll!!!!!!!!!!!!!!!!!!!!

Two goals in the World Cup final – Phil was now officially a national hero! As he spun away to celebrate, the whole squad chased after him.

'Yes, you legend!'

'We've done it – we've won the World Cup!'

At the final whistle, the Spanish players dropped to the grass in despair, while the Young Lions roared with pride. England were the new Under-17 World Champions! After lots of team hugs and photos, the players went up one by one to collect their winners' medals, and then at last it was trophy time.

Ohhhhhhhhhhhhhhhhhhhh...

...Hurrrraaaaaaaaaaaaayyyyy!

As the England captains Joel Latibeaudiere and Angel lifted the trophy high into the sky, Phil was right behind them, bouncing up and down with a big grin on his face.

Campeones, Campeones, Olé! Olé! Olé!

What a night, and what a tournament! Not only had he helped his team to win the World Cup, but Phil had also won the prestigious Golden Ball award for Best Player. The list of previous winners included idols like Toni Kroos and Cesc Fàbregas. Wow! Surely, there was no stopping Phil now.

CHAPTER 12

FIRST STEPS AS A SENIOR CITY PLAYER

'What position did Phil Foden play?' Guardiola joked at a press conference just hours after England's World Cup Under-17 World Cup victory. 'Because when he comes back, I'm going to put him in this position, if he scores two goals in the final!'

The City manager was full of praise for his young star, and he wasn't the only one talking about Phil's return to the club. Vincent, the captain, tweeted, 'get yourself home, we've got a game on Wednesday!'

Sadly, Phil wasn't back in time to play in that match, but three weeks later, he was named as one of the substitutes for City's Champions League match against Feyenoord. While it was exciting news, he didn't want to get his hopes up just yet. He had been on the bench before against Celtic, and that time, he hadn't played a single second...

With twenty minutes to go at the Etihad, the score against Feyenoord was still 0–0. What would Guardiola do next? He had already brought on Gabriel Jesus in attack, but that wasn't enough; the team needed another burst of fresh energy. David Silva? Brahim? No, the manager went for his new Under-17 World Cup winner instead; he was ready to become a first-team player.

'Phil, get warmed up – you're coming on!' one of the coaches called out.

His opportunity had arrived; he was about to make his City debut! Phil removed his warm-up bib and tracksuit top in a hurry to reveal the sky-blue City shirt underneath with his new number on the back – 47, in memory of his beloved granddad, Walter. He was determined to make him and the rest of his family proud.

As he waited on the touchline for Yaya to walk off, Phil took a deep breath to compose himself and a second to enjoy the moment. It had been his dream since the age of five to play first-team football for City, and now it was coming true. First winning the Under-17s World Cup and now this – what a month he was having! Right, time to shine. He jogged onto the pitch and straight into the action.

'YES!' he called for the ball, and when it came, he calmly controlled it, turned and passed it on. Easy! Phil looked like an experienced star out there already, rather than City's new record-breaking star. Yes, at the age of years and 177 days, he had just become the club's youngest ever Champions League debutant!

For those final fifteen minutes, Phil didn't stop running. When his team had the ball, he sprinted into space and then passed and moved, passed and moved his way up the pitch. And when the other team had it, he worked hard to win the ball back. The fans loved Phil's lively, positive style, but could he help City to grab a winning goal? In the eighty-eighth minute, Raheem Sterling played a one-two with İlkay Gündoğan and then chipped the ball over the keeper. *1–0!*

'YESSSSSSSSSSSSSSSSS!' Phil yelled out as he raced over to join Raheem and the rest of his teammates in front of the celebrating supporters. At last, City were winning, and he was so proud to be a part of it.

At the final whistle, Phil walked around the pitch, swapping high-fives with his teammates, clapping the fans, and waving to his family and friends in the crowd. He was buzzing with so much excitement that he didn't want his debut night to ever end!

So, what next for City's new homegrown hero? More record-breaking moments! A few weeks later, in their final group game against Shakhtar Donetsk, Phil became the youngest English player ever to start a match in the Champions League. Although they lost 2–1 and Guardiola asked him to play as a left wing-back, Phil was still one of City's star performers and stayed on for the full ninety minutes.

'Foden is the Future!' one journalist declared afterwards.

Phil had a lot to live up to after leading England to World Cup glory, but he was handling the pressure brilliantly. Step by step, he was pushing his way into the City first team, and soon, it was time for his Premier League debut. In mid-December, with City beating Tottenham 3–0 at home at the Etihad, Phil ran on to replace İlkay for the last ten minutes. Another dream ticked off!

Phil was far too busy to stop and let his achievements sink in, though. The next night, he added the BBC Young Sports Personality of the Year award to his growing trophy cabinet, and two nights after that, he was part of the City team which beat Leicester on penalties in the League Cup quarter-finals.

What a whirlwind few days! Things were moving so fast for Phil – a little too fast, in fact. In the last minutes of the quarter-final, he had to limp off with a foot injury, and he ended up missing over two months of football. Nooooooo, what a nightmare! It was the first serious injury of Phil's career, but he didn't let it get him down. He worked hard on his recovery and when he returned, he looked better than ever.

In his first game back, Phil set up Sergio to score – his first Premier League assist!

Two weeks later, he came on for the last few

minutes of City's League Cup final win over Arsenal – yes, his first senior trophy!

And on the final day of the season against Southampton, he played his fifth match to earn a Premier League winner's medal – hurray, his first league title, and he was also the new youngest player ever to win it!

Despite all the talk, the trophies and the incredible records, however, Phil wasn't getting carried away. He hadn't even scored his first senior goal yet! He knew that he still had a long way to go in his football career, with lots to learn and lots to achieve. Although it was amazing to have a Premier League winner's medal already, he didn't really feel like he had done enough to deserve it. So, he joined the squad for the open-top bus celebrations through the streets of Manchester, but when Vincent invited him to the team party, Phil said, 'Thanks, but I'm going fishing with my dad instead.'

CHAPTER 13

PATIENCE AND PROGRESS

After a few weeks off, fishing with his dad, playing football with his mates in Stockport, and watching football at the 2018 World Cup in Russia, Phil couldn't wait for City's preseason training to start. His first season had been a success, and now he was hungry for more – more games, more goals, more assists. That wasn't going to be easy at a top team like City, but Phil was 'one of their own' and he was determined to become a club legend. So, what could he do to push for a starting place?

1) Work hard on his weaknesses

On top of the team training sessions, Phil also hired a running coach to help improve his sprint speed. The hours of ladder drills and high-knee exercises were exhausting, but he was an eager learner, and he could soon see the results. By taking shorter steps and using his arms to push him forward, Phil was getting faster and faster!

2) Show his commitment to the club

In July, Phil was called up to the England Under-19s squad for the European Championships in Finland, but in the end, he decided not to go. Why? Because if he went, he would miss City's trip to the USA. As he had seen the previous year, the preseason tour was a great chance to impress his manager, especially as a lot of the senior players were still on holiday after the World Cup. So if Pep wanted him to stay with City, then that's what he would do!

Phil also felt like he would develop more at the International Champions Cup, where he would get to test himself against older and better players from three of the biggest clubs in the world. City lost against both Borussia Dortmund and Liverpool, but in their final match, they fought back from 2–0 to beat Bayern Munich 3–2.

What a win! The whole team played brilliantly, but Phil was certainly one of the stand-out stars. He set up the first goal for Bernardo Silva just before half-time, and then early in the second half, he went for the shot himself. His powerful strike was saved by the keeper, but the rebound fell at Lukas Nmecha's feet.

'Phil Foden was excellent,' Pep said after the game. 'He never gives up and I like that.'

3) Make the most of his opportunities

After another impressive preseason, Guardiola gave Phil the chance to start in the FA Community Shield against Chelsea. Wow, what an opportunity, and it only took him ten minutes to make a massive impact.

As Bernardo collected the ball on the halfway line, Phil burst into the pocket of space behind the Chelsea midfield. DANGER ALERT! When the pass arrived, he dribbled forward and as the defenders backed away, he kept on going. On the edge of the penalty area, Phil finally passed the ball to Sergio, who fired it into the bottom corner. 1–0!

'Thanks, mate!' Sergio screamed as the City players celebrated together.

Early in the second half, Phil set up Sergio again with a beautiful through-ball, but his shot went wide. Never mind – a few minutes later, the striker got another chance and scored. *2–0!*

City had already won their first trophy of the season, and Phil was so proud to have played a crucial part. This time as the players celebrated on the balcony at Wembley, he really felt like he belonged there alongside club legends like Vincent and Sergio.

But was Phil now ready to become a regular starter in the Premier League? According to Pep, the answer was yes. 'He was ready last season and now one year on he's more mature,' the City manager said after the match.

Phil, however, would have to be patient because City started the new season in style, going fifteen games unbeaten! With Sergio and Raheem scoring the goals and the two Silvas, David and Bernardo, running the show in midfield, Phil was lucky if he got off the bench at all in the Premier League.

Oh well, he would just have to shine in the cup competitions instead for now. In the League Cup against Oxford, Phil set up City's second goal with a defence-splitting pass to Riyad Mahrez. *ASSIST!*

Then in the final seconds, Raheem slipped the ball to Phil inside the penalty area. It was Phil's best chance yet to score his first senior goal for City, and he wasn't going to waste it. He let the ball roll across to his left foot and then fired it first-time into the bottom corner. *3–0!*

Gooooooooooooooooooaaaaaaaaaaaaaaaalllllllllllllllllllllllllll!!!!!!!!!!!!!!!!!!!!!!

Yessssss, he was off the mark at last! Phil had been dreaming about this moment for so many years, and now it had finally arrived. He threw his arms out wide and slid towards the corner flag on his knees. Then as he knelt there in front of the cheering fans, he lifted his shirt to his lips and kissed the City badge. What an unbelievable feeling!

A few months later in the FA Cup, Phil was at it again, scoring one against Rotherham and then two against Newport County.

'Go on, Pep,' the City supporters urged their manager. 'Give him a proper chance in the Premier

League!'

But by the end of January 2019, Phil still hadn't started a single league match.

4) Keep learning from his heroes

Some young footballers in Phil's position might have grown frustrated and moved on to another club. His friend Jadon, for example, had gone to Germany to get more game-time and he was already one of Borussia Dortmund's star players. That season, he had played well over 1,000 minutes in the Bundesliga, whereas Phil had played fewer than one hundred minutes in the Premier League.

What about going out on loan for the rest of the season? Tottenham and Everton were both interested in him, but no, Phil wasn't going anywhere. He was determined to stay and succeed at City, his club since he was a kid. He knew that he still had a lot of improvements to make if he wanted to break into the starting line-up, but he was in the best possible place to grow.

Every day, he was working hard with Pep, the best coach in the world, who believed in him and wanted to help him become a better player. And every day, he was practising with world-class players like Raheem, Sergio, Kevin, Bernardo, and best of all, 'The Master'.

That's what Phil called David Silva, his favourite player of all. Ever since his very first training session with the City first team, Phil had been trying to learn as much as possible from 'The Master'.

Why did he make certain runs?

How did he spot certain passes and spaces?

How was he able to see things before they even happened?

What tips did he have for keeping hold of the ball in really tight spaces, especially when you're not very big?

David was a quiet, humble guy, but he was always happy to help Phil and pass on his football knowledge. Perhaps one day soon Phil would be the player to replace David in the centre of the City midfield. Yes, that was the goal that Phil was working towards.

CHAPTER 14

A PROPER PREMIER LEAGUE PLAYER NOW

But how long would Phil have to wait for a proper chance at City? Between December 2018 and February 2019, he was permitted fewer than twenty minutes playing in the Premier League, and he was left on the bench as City won the League Cup final against Chelsea.

'There's no rush – you're still only eighteen,' Phil kept telling himself but he was desperate to play.

In early April, his patience and progress were finally rewarded. With a Champions League quarter-final coming up, Guardiola decided to rest the two Silvas for their Premier League match against Cardiff City. That left a space alongside Fernandinho and Kevin in midfield, a Phil-sized pocket of space.

At last, his first Premier League start! With a proud smile on his face, Phil walked out onto the Etihad pitch and tried to enjoy every single touch. He was living his dream and he wanted to be on the ball as much as possible. Pass and move, pass and move, tackles, interceptions, skilful dribbles, and lots of shots – it was another all-action performance from 'The Stockport Iniesta'.

Early in the second half, Phil burst into the box past the Cardiff defence, but the keeper rushed out and blocked his shot. *So close!*

Moments later, Leroy Sané whipped in a dangerous corner and Phil reacted brilliantly to volley the ball goalwards, but it crashed back off the post. *So unlucky!*

With his hands on his head and his mouth open wide, Phil turned away in disbelief. Never mind, the most important things were that City had won and he had made a fantastic full Premier League debut. Another dream achieved! Onto the next one...

Pep was so impressed with Phil's performance that

he picked him to start again two weeks later in one of City's biggest battles of the season. With four games to go, they were just one point above Liverpool at the top of the Premier League table. Every match was a must-win now, especially this one against Tottenham, the team who only three days earlier had knocked them out of the Champions League.

It was a chance for City to get instant revenge, and they came out flying right from kick-off. In the fifth minute, Bernardo cut inside off the right wing and chipped a high cross towards Sergio at the back post. The angle was too tight for him to try and score himself, so instead Sergio headed it back across the six-yard box to… Phil! He had cleverly drifted into space between the Tottenham centre-backs and he threw himself forward towards the ball, meeting it with a diving header. *1–0!*

Goooooooooooooooooooaaaaaaaaaaaaaaaalllllllllllllll llllllllll!!!!!!!!!!!!!!!!!!

As he landed face-first in the net, Phil heard the Etihad Stadium erupt all around him. He had done it; with his first-ever Premier League goal, he had just given City the lead in a very important game! In a flash, he picked himself up and raced over to celebrate with Sergio and Bernardo.

'Come onnnnnnnnn!' Phil roared, punching the air with passion. In that amazing moment, he felt absolutely invincible.

Eighty-five tense minutes later, that goal turned out to be the winner. Yes, thanks to his diving header, City had their revenge and they were still top of the Premier League table!

Phil made sure that he enjoyed his moment as the match-winner. While he listened to the supporters chant his name, he clapped and smiled until his hands and face hurt. What a feeling – as a kid, he had sat there in the crowd, cheering for his heroes, and now the fans were cheering for him!

Phil was one of the last players to leave the pitch and when he did eventually walk down the tunnel, he had to go and do TV interviews straight away. Bernardo won the *Sky Sports Man of the Match* award, but when Phil was asked to present it to him, Bernardo gave it straight back.

'I'd like to hand it over to Phil because I honestly think he deserves it,' the Portuguese midfielder said, patting him on the back. 'He's so young and he's a fantastic player.'

Cheers, Bernardo! Phil really felt like a key part of the first-team squad now, as well as a proper Premier League player. So when City held on to win the title for the second season in a row, he was able to lift the trophy with a real sense of satisfaction. He deserved this one, especially after his big-game goal against Tottenham.

'BACK 2 BACK!' Phil posted on social media alongside a photo of pure joy in sky blue. He was so glad that he had stayed at City and he was already looking forward to next season.

First, however, Phil was off to spend the summer in Italy and San Marino, starring for England at the Under-21 European Championships.

CHAPTER 15

MORE GOALS, MORE ASSISTS

When he received the ball from James Maddison near the halfway line, Phil spun beautifully and looked up for an England teammate to pass to. He could see Ryan Sessegnon on the left, but there was an opponent in the way, so Phil decided to go it alone instead.

With a burst of speed, he glided between two France midfielders, and then with two perfect touches of the ball in a very tight space, he glided past two more! Phil was on the edge of the penalty area now, with four defenders surrounding him, but there was no stopping him. He dribbled forward and then with a sudden drop of the shoulder, he shifted the ball to the

left, opening up just enough room for a shot. BANG! It
wasn't a particularly powerful strike, but it didn't have
to be because it was so accurate. The ball rolled past
the stunned keeper and into the bottom corner. *1–0!*

*Goooooooooooooooooooaaaaaaaaaaaaaaaaalllllllllllllll
lllllllllllll!!!!!!!!!!!!!!!!!!!!!!!*

Wow, what a way to give England the lead! At first,
Phil tried to play it cool and just jog away, but no, he
couldn't stay calm after scoring one of his greatest
goals ever. With the adrenaline rushing through his
body, he suddenly raced over to the sidelines as his
teammates chased after him.

'Mate, that was unbelievable – you're a genius!'
James shouted, throwing his arms around England's
hero.

Unfortunately, Phil's sensational strike wasn't
enough to secure the victory. In the last minutes,
France fought back to equalise and then win 2–1.
Nooooooooooo! As he watched Aaron Wan-Bissaka's
clearance loop up and land in his own net, Phil threw
his hands to his head in disbelief.

Despite Phil's best efforts, it turned out to be a

disastrous Euros for the England Under-21s. With a
4–2 defeat against Romania, they crashed out of the
tournament in the group stage.

It was a big disappointment for Phil after his glory
days with the Under-17s, but he soon had good news
to cheer him up. His City manager had been talking
about him, and when he heard what Guardiola had
said, Phil was blown away:

'He is the most talented player I've ever seen as a
football player and manager.'

Wow, really? That was a massive statement from
someone who had worked with Messi, Neymar Jr,
Iniesta, and Robert Lewandowski! But whether he
was telling the truth or not, Pep's words gave Phil lots
of confidence ahead of the 2019–20 season campaign.
He felt like he was reaching a very important point in
his City career, especially as 'The Master' would soon
be moving on.

After ten years at the club, David Silva had recently
announced that he would be leaving at the end of the
season. Phil had learned so much from his teammate
and he was really going to miss playing with him,

but The Master's departure would open up a space in midfield, and he was determined to grab it. City didn't need to sign someone new to replace David; they already had Kevin, İlkay, Bernardo and Phil. Yes, he was ready to prove that he was as great as Guardiola said he was.

Phil's season started in the same way as the last – with an impressive preseason tour, followed by victory in the Community Shield. This time, he only came on in the last minute against Liverpool, but when the match went to penalties, he bravely stepped up to score, sending Alisson the wrong way. *GOAL!*

Phil didn't celebrate, or even smile; he just jogged back to the halfway like it was no big deal. It was only moments later, once City were the winners, that he let his emotions show.

Hurraaaaaaaaaay!!!

A seventh club trophy was a great way to kick off what Phil hoped would be a breakthrough year for him at City. He was aiming to play more matches, and also to make more key contributions to the team: more goals like his worldie against France and his spot-kick against Liverpool, and more assists too. Those were the things that he needed to add in order to take his game to the next level.

In the Champions League, he only came on for the last few minutes at home against Dinamo Zagreb, but he still managed to score. As City counter-attacked, Raheem played the ball through to Phil and he calmly guided it into the bottom corner with his weaker right foot. *GOAL!*

In their next match against Atalanta, Phil returned the favour, setting up Raheem for a simple tap-in. *ASSIST!*

Then, away in Zagreb, Phil celebrated his fiftieth appearance for City by setting up one for Gabriel Jesus and scoring one himself. *GOAL AND ASSIST!*

'Come onnnnn!' he roared up at the sky. Phil could feel himself getting better and better, and closer and closer to a regular starting spot. He just had to keep doing what he was doing.

In the League Cup quarter-final against Oxford United, Phil played a beautiful pass to put João Cancelo through on goal. *ASSIST!*

In the FA Cup third round against Port Vale, İlkay chipped the ball through to Phil, and he had the confidence and technique to volley it straight across to Sergio. *ASSIST!*

Later on, Phil raced from the halfway line to the six-yard box to slide home City's fourth. *GOAL!*

'Yesssssss!' he cried out as he leapt up and punched the air. Another game, another two key contributions!

But what about Phil's Premier League appearances? Sadly, he still wasn't starting many games, but when he did get the chance, he made the most of it. Away at Arsenal, his pass launched the attack that led to City's second goal, and he also slipped the ball through to Kevin for the third. *ANOTHER ASSIST!*

'Thanks, what a pass!' Kevin cheered, giving Phil a high-five and a hug.

No problem! That's what he was in the Manchester City team to do.

CHAPTER 16

MANCHESTER CITY'S MAN OF THE FINAL

1 March 2020, Wembley Stadium

Manchester City were in the League Cup final for the third year in a row, but for Phil, this one was going to be different. Because after being a late sub in 2018, and then staying on the bench in 2019, he had made it into Guardiola's starting line-up in 2020! When he found out the news the day before in training, Phil was buzzing with excitement. It meant so much to know that his manager trusted him in such a big match. Watch out Aston Villa – Phil was fired up and ready to shine for the full ninety minutes!

As he warmed up on the pitch at Wembley, Phil

couldn't wait for the game to begin. Not only was he about to take part in a big cup final in front of over 80,000 fans, but he also had a new, more attacking role to play. Pep had picked Rodri, İlkay and David in midfield, with Phil pushing further forward in a front three alongside Sergio and Raheem. What a dream team!

After the handshakes and the national anthem, at last it was time for kick-off. In the first few minutes, Phil rushed around the field, desperate to get his first touch. When it arrived, he made sure that it was a good one. As Matt Targett slid in, Phil steered the ball around him, skipped the tackle and kept going, past Marvelous Nakamba, and past Douglas Luiz too.

'Yessssssss!' the City supporters roared as their homegrown hero carried the ball forward.

Phil's rampaging run ended with a corner-kick, and that was just the beginning for City's bright young star. In the twentieth minute, as Rodri collected the ball in the middle, Phil burst from the right wing into the box. As the pass flew towards him, he had some quick decisions to make.

Should he chest it down or try to volley it? No, the ball was too high for either of those options – it would have to be a header.

Should he go for goal himself? No, the angle was too tight for that and he was a little off balance anyway. Plus, Phil could see City's striker sprinting into the six-yard box…

With a flick of his head, he nodded the ball down to Sergio, who swept it past the keeper. *1–0!*

'Come onnnnnnn!' Phil cried out. City had scored in the League Cup final, and he had helped set it up! As an eleven-year-old, he had watched Sergio win City their first Premier League title, and now eight years later, here they were hugging each other and running together towards the fans by the corner flag. Unbelievable!

A few minutes later, Phil almost grabbed a goal to go with his assist. When Oleksandr Zinchenko moved the play from left to right with a long diagonal ball, he controlled it beautifully, cut inside on his left foot and fired a shot that swerved just wide of the far post.

'Ooooooooo!' he gasped with his hands over his

MATT AND TOM OLDFIELD

mouth. So close!

Phil was on fire and he didn't want the first half to end. One second, he was chasing back to win the ball off Jack Grealish, and the next he was playing one-twos with Kyle and İlkay and almost setting up another goal for Sergio. What a superstar!

In the second half, the Villa tackles got stronger and stronger, but they still couldn't stop him. Phil skipped away from Targett again and again, leaving the left-back trailing behind. And as well as dribbling past his opponents, he also showed the vision to play defence-splitting balls. In the sixtieth minute, Phil spotted Kevin on the run and slipped a sublime pass through to him. His cross was heading straight to Sergio, until Tyrone Mings slid in at the last second to block it. As he watched on, Phil threw his hands to his head – so close again!

In the end, it didn't matter because City held on for a 2–1 win. At the final whistle, Phil fell to the floor, exhausted and emotional. Trophy number eight! His club had won the League Cup yet again, and he was so proud of his own performance: the energy, the

107

quality, and of course, the assist. Pep had put his faith in him, and Phil had delivered big time in a big game.

'Well done, you were incredible today!' his manager congratulated him, wrapping him in a hug.

Later on, as David the captain led his team up the steps to the Wembley balcony to collect the trophy, who was the player right behind him? Phil! Yes, at last he felt like he had earned his place amongst City's superstars. He was one of them now, and he belonged on the biggest stage. With the medal hanging around his neck, Phil stood there soaking up the amazing atmosphere and waiting for the most exciting moment.

'The Carabao Cup 2020 goes to...' the loudspeakers announced, '...MANCHESTER CITY!'

Hurrrraaaaaaaaaaaaaayyyyy!

As the confetti whirled around them, Phil bounced up and down with delight. What a day, and it wasn't over yet. On top of the medal and the League Cup, he had also become the youngest ever winner of the Alan Hardaker Trophy, awarded to the man of the match. After a few years of patient progress, Phil's time had finally come.

CHAPTER 17

TAKING OVER FROM THE MASTER

Phil's big breakthrough moment had arrived – a new City superstar was born! In the days to come, however, he would have to show patience again, although for a very different reason. Just two weeks after City's League Cup win, the Premier League season was suspended due to the COVID-19 pandemic. It was a very difficult and uncertain time for everyone. How long would the lockdown last, and when would it be safe to start mixing with other people again? No-one really knew the answers.

'God, I miss football,' Phil tweeted with a video of him juggling a toilet roll. He loved the game so much that even now that he was a famous Manchester City first-team star, he was still happy to play anytime, anywhere, and with whatever he could find.

At last in late May, Premier League teams were allowed to start training again, and in mid-June, the season resumed. Hurray! So, could Phil pick up where he left off with that League Cup final performance? Oh yes, he could!

Against Arsenal, he replaced David with thirty minutes to go and raced forward on the counter-attack to make it 3–0 to City.

Goooooooooooooooooooooaaaaaaaaaaaaaaaaalllllllllllllll llllllllllll!!!!!!!!!!!!!!!!!!!!!

'Amazing to be back,' Phil posted on social media after the match.

Five days later, he started on the left wing against Burnley and scored two more. One was a brilliant low, fizzing strike from just outside the box, and the other was a tap-in at the back post.

Goooooooooooooooooooooaaaaaaaaaaaaaaaaalllllllllllllll llllllllllll!!!!!!!!!!!!!!!!!!!!!

Goooooooooooooooooooooaaaaaaaaaaaaaaaaalllllllllllllll llllllllllll!!!!!!!!!!!!!!!!!!!!!

Three goals in two games! With a quick punch of the air, Phil jogged over to thank Gabriel for the flick-on. It was a really strange feeling celebrating in an empty stadium, but he was still delighted to be scoring regularly for City. And he wasn't just grabbing goals for himself; he was also creating chances for others. Against Burnley, his cross to Sergio led to a penalty, and then his unbelievable, no-look pass to Bernardo helped set up the fourth goal for David.

'Thanks, what a ball!' The Master said with a beaming smile.

Phil had worked so hard to earn his place in the starting line-up, and now, thanks to his fantastic form, he was there to stay. And while, like David, his preferred position was still definitely in the middle of midfield, he was happy to play wherever Pep asked him to, as long as it helped the team to win.

For City, there would be no third league title in a row, however. Phil was rested for their next game against Chelsea and they lost 2–1 without him, which handed the trophy to their rivals, Liverpool. Nooooooooooo! For the City players, it was always disappointing to finish second in anything, but two weeks later, they sent out a warning to the new Premier League champions: we'll be back next season, and better than ever.

Kevin scored from the spot after a foul on Raheem. *1–0!*

On the counter-attack, İlkay played the ball up to Gabriel, who passed it right to Phil, who dribbled forward and slipped it left to Raheem. *2–0!*

Just before half-time, Phil played a one-two with Kevin and raced into the box, where he fired a shot past Alisson. *3–0!*

Goooooooooooooooooooooaaaaaaaaaaaaaaaaaallllllllllllll llllllllllll!!!!!!!!!!!!!!!!!!!!!

Phil slid towards the corner flag on his knees and clenched his fist. That was more like it! When they moved the ball that quickly and cleverly, City were unstoppable. That night, after the match, he wrote a message to their rivals: 'Congratulations to Liverpool for this year but we definitely showed we're ready for next season!!'

Before that, however, it was time for City to say

goodbye to 'The Master'. After ten magical years in
the team, they were going to miss David's vision and
skill so much. But didn't they already have a ready-
made replacement, the wonderkid they called 'The
Stockport Iniesta'? According to Pep, the answer was
yes:

'When David said it was his last year, I told the
board we have Phil, so we don't have to invest. In the
next decade, or fifteen years, he will be an outstanding
player for us. I don't have doubts.'

Wow, what a wonderful thing to hear! Phil couldn't
wait for the start of the 2020–21 Premier League
season. On the opening day away at Wolves, there
was his name on the City teamsheet, next to Rodri,
Fernandinho and Kevin. Yes – from now on, Phil was
going to be a first-team regular!

City started strongly and their little Number 47 was
at the centre of everything. From wide on the right
wing, Phil slid a perfect pass into Kevin's path, as he
raced into the box. *FOUL, PENALTY, 1–0!*

Then in the thirtieth minute, City scored again
with a stunning team move: Rodri to Phil, forward to

Gabriel, back to Kevin, through to Raheem, and then across to Phil to finish it off. *2–0!*

Goooooooooooooooooooooaaaaaaaaaaaaaaaaaallllllllllllll llllllllllll!!!!!!!!!!!!!!!!!!

What a beautiful piece of flowing, passing football! On the sidelines, their manager looked ecstatic, and as he high-fived his teammates, Phil knew that it was a move that 'The Master' himself would have been proud of too.

He had big boots to fill, but so far, Phil looked like the perfect fit. The vision, the skill, the goals, the assists – there was no stopping him now that he was a City superstar, as well as a senior England international.

CHAPTER 18

ENGLAND HIGHS AND LOWS

From winning the World Cup with the Under-17s to scoring that wonder goal against France for the Under-21s – Phil had already shown that he had the quality to shine for England. So surely it was only a matter of time before he was starring for the senior team too?

The manager, Gareth Southgate, had been following his progress for years, but he wanted Phil to get more first-team experience at City first. Mission accomplished! With his breakthrough game in the League Cup final against Aston Villa and his Premier League performances against Burnley and Liverpool, Phil had proved himself at the highest level. So in August 2020, Southgate phoned Phil with some very welcome news: it was time for him to step up to the senior squad!

'An honour to be called up!' Phil tweeted with great excitement. 'Can't wait to pull that England shirt on!!'

It was a very proud moment for him and for his whole family. His grandad Walter had been right all along; Phil would play for England one day!

But when would that special day come, when he would make his senior international debut? England were playing two UEFA Nations League matches in four days, away in Iceland and then Denmark. With so little time between games, Southgate would need to use his full squad, perhaps even the four uncapped players including Phil.

What an opportunity! Phil was determined to make the most of it. So what if he was one of the new kids? He was fired up and full of self-belief. By working hard at the team training camp, Phil hoped to impress his manager and get the chance to play at least a few minutes of football.

After a neat one-two with James Ward-Prowse, he fired a shot past Conor Coady's outstretched leg and into Dean Henderson's bottom corner. *GOAL!*

'Brilliant, Phil!' the England coaches clapped and cheered.

A few days later, when Southgate named his team for the first match against Iceland, Phil wasn't on the subs bench; he was in the starting line-up instead! And not only that but Phil was also in his favourite midfield playmaker role behind a front three of:

The captain Harry Kane,

His City teammate Raheem,

And his old City academy teammate Jadon.

Wow, what a dream come true! Wearing the Number 11 shirt, Phil walked out onto the pitch in Reykjavik to make his England debut. Sadly, there were still no supporters allowed in the stadium because of the coronavirus, but even that couldn't spoil Phil's special night.

'Let's gooooo!' he shouted as he shared a high-five with Jadon.

Although Phil's debut did end in a victory for England, unfortunately he had already left the field by the time the winning goal was scored. For sixty-eight minutes, he passed and moved, passed and moved around the pitch, just like he did so well at City. But for once, he couldn't quite find that killer ball to break through the defence.

'Well played,' Southgate said to Phil as he made his way off towards the bench. 'It's not easy to find space out there, but you looked like you'd been doing this for years!'

Phew! Phil smiled with relief at his manager's reassuring words. Next time, he would be better; he had no doubt about that. For now, though, he was officially an England international, and that was an incredible feeling.

'I've been dreaming of this day ever since I was [a] little kid,' Phil posted on social media that night. 'It was an honour to represent my country tonight and I can't wait to push on and play more!!'

Phil was hoping for more game-time in the next match against Denmark, but unfortunately, there was trouble ahead. After the thrill of making his England debut, Phil was in the mood to celebrate, and so he was one of two players who made the foolish decision to break the COVID-19 rules and leave the team area of the hotel. Uh-oh! When Southgate found out the next day, he sent both players home in disgrace.

Noooooo, what a stupid mistake, what a wasted opportunity! Phil was furious with himself for letting everyone down like that: his manager, his teammates, the supporters, his club, his family. Everyone! Yes, he was still a young player, but there was no excuse for bad behaviour. He had learned a valuable lesson, and it would never happen again. A long apology wasn't going to make things right, but it was a start. Then Phil worked harder than ever at City to force his way back into the England team...

In the Premier League against West Ham, Phil controlled the bouncing ball beautifully, spun and shot past the keeper. *GOAL!*

In the Champions League against Porto, he set up Ferran Torres with a perfectly weighted pass. *ASSIST!*

Phil wasn't selected for the next four England matches, but by November, he had successfully worked his way into Southgate's squad again.

'So good to be back!' Phil tweeted after arriving at

training camp.

Right, no more mistakes; it was time to really shine for England at senior level. The first game against Ireland was already won when he came on for the last thirty minutes, and he stayed on the bench for the defeat to Belgium, but at Wembley against Iceland, Southgate finally gave Phil another chance to start. And this time, he did everything right for England.

In the first half, he curled a dangerous free kick into the box, where Declan Rice scored with his shoulder. *1–0!* Phil's first senior England assist!

And in the second half, he raced into the box to collect Jadon's pass and sweep the ball into the bottom corner. *3–0!* Phil's first senior England goal!

Four minutes later, he fired in a second from just outside the box. *4–0!*

What a performance and what a feeling! The proud smile didn't leave Phil's face for days. Hurray, he was back to being an England hero again! And his timing was perfect because Euro 2020 was only seven months away.

CHAPTER 19

UNSTOPPABLE CITY

Phil returned home to Manchester feeling more motivated than ever. He knew that the best way to secure a spot in England's Euro 2020 squad was to keep starring for City – more goals, more assists, and more glory. Every year, the club challenged for all the top trophies: the League Cup, the Premier League, the FA Cup, and the greatest prize of all, the Champions League. So, could this be the season when they finally did the Quadruple? Phil was going to give it his best shot.

City had won the League Cup for the last three years in a row, and they were the favourites to lift the trophy again in 2021. Phil set up one and scored the other as they beat Bournemouth in the Third Round, and he was the star of the show again as they thrashed Arsenal in the quarter-finals.

Phil passed it wide to Oleksandr, who crossed it to Gabriel. *1–0!*

In the second half, Phil burst into the space between the Arsenal right-back and centre-back, and when the ball arrived, he skilfully flicked it over the outrushing keeper. *3–1!*

Goooooooooooooooooooooaaaaaaaaaaaaaaaaalllllllllllllll llllllllllll!!!!!!!!!!!!!!!!!!!!!

'What a finish!' Fernandinho shouted, lifting him high into the air.

Fifteen minutes later, Phil capped off an incredible performance by chipping in a cross for Aymeric Laporte to head home. *4–1!*

In the semi-finals, City faced United in a big Manchester derby. The Foden family was divided as usual, but their boy helped make sure the city stayed blue.

Phil's fizzing free kick was bundled in by John Stones. *1–0!*

Fernandinho volleyed in from long range. *2–0!*

And with that, unstoppable City were through to yet another League Cup final. Their first trophy of the season was in sight, but could they lift the Premier League title too?

After a poor start to the season, City were getting back to their best, thanks to a tactical switch by Guardiola. With Sergio injured and Gabriel struggling to score, the manager had made the brave decision to play without any strikers at all. Instead, the forwards took it in turns to act as a 'false nine': Raheem, Kevin, Bernardo, Riyad, Ferran and Phil.

'Foden up front? No way, he's tiny – the defenders will destroy him!'

At first, the fans worried about where the goals would come from, but there was no need; Pep's plan worked perfectly. With their amazing passing and movement, City tore through team after team, winning game after game, and the players shared the scoring around.

Raheem was the hero against Southampton…

Then İlkay and Ferran against Newcastle…

...And away at Chelsea, İlkay, Phil and Kevin all got one goal each.

From the left wing, Phil sprinted forward into the pocket of space between the right-back and the centre-back. DANGER ALERT! It didn't matter that he was smaller than the defenders when he made such intelligent runs. Kevin's first pass didn't quite reach him, but his second attempt did, and with a clever sweep of his left foot, Phil guided the ball into the gap at Edouard Mendy's near post.

Gooooooooooooooooooooaaaaaaaaaaaaaaaaalllllllllllllll llllllllllll!!!!!!!!!!!!!!!!!!!!

Wow, what quick-thinking! It was Phil's third Premier League goal of the season and a really important one too against their Top Six rivals. 'Yessssssssss!' he cried out as he hugged Kevin. He was so proud to be part of such a special team.

While the clubs around them slipped up, City stayed strong. At the back, John and Ruben Dias had formed an unbeatable partnership, and in attack, Pep had so many forward options to choose from that one of them was always sure to score. Against Brighton,

Bernardo hit the post and Raheem missed a penalty, but City never stopped believing they would win eventually...

İlkay to Kevin, to Phil, to Bernardo, back to Kevin, then through to Phil on the run! He had two defenders in front of him, but with one silky touch Phil skipped away from both of them. As another defender closed in, he was forced to shoot fast and with his weaker right foot. No problem, it was just as accurate.

Goooooooooooooooooooooaaaaaaaaaaaaaaaaallllllllllllllll lllllllllllll!!!!!!!!!!!!!!!!!!!!

'Come onnnnnnnnn!' Phil yelled as he jumped up and punched the air. When his team needed him most, he had stepped up to score another big-game goal.

'Yes mate, you hero!' John cheered with joy and relief.

The win lifted City above Liverpool and into second place, just one point behind their Manchester rivals United.

'We keep going!' Phil posted on social media after

the match, and that's exactly what they did:

Manchester City 4 Crystal Palace 0,

It was Phil's turn to cheer for John, as the centre-back scored twice. 'Who needs a striker when we've got you?!' he joked as they bumped fists together.

Manchester City 2 Aston Villa 0,

Bernardo and Ruben both missed sitters and João Cancelo hit the bar, but eventually the goals arrived. First, Bernardo curled a beauty into the top corner, and then İlkay scored from the penalty spot.

'Get in!' Phil shouted, throwing his arms up in the air. What wonderful teammates he had! They never gave up, no matter what.

West Brom 0 Manchester City 5,

Manchester City 1 Sheffield United 0,

Burnley 0 Manchester City 2...

With nine league wins in a row, they were top of the table again at last. Could they make it ten by beating the reigning champions at Anfield? It wouldn't be easy, but Phil was feeling confident. He had starred against Liverpool before, and City looked unstoppable.

CHAPTER 20

PHIL, THE FALSE NINE

7 February 2021, Anfield

'Let's do this!' Phil shouted, sharing a quick high-five with John before kick-off. Liverpool versus Manchester City, the reigning champions against the future champions – Phil had been waiting for this fixture all season. City hadn't won a Premier League match at Anfield since 2003, and they wouldn't get a better chance than this. Liverpool had just been beaten by Brighton and they had no Virgil van Dijk, no Joël Matip, and no fans in the stadium cheering them on.

What an opportunity! Phil was ready to play a key part in a famous City victory. With Kevin out injured and Bernardo deeper in midfield, it was his turn to play the false nine role, flanked by Raheem on the left and Riyad on the right. It was another new position for Phil to get used to, Pep trusted his talent and intelligence to shine anywhere on the pitch. And as the game went on, City's young star got better and better.

As a false nine, Phil didn't have to stay up front like a normal striker; he had the freedom to move around and make it difficult for defenders to mark him. Early in the second half, he dropped deep to collect the ball from İlkay and spread it wide to Raheem on the left wing. Then he quietly crept his way into the middle, and into the small pocket of space between the Liverpool midfield and defence...

'Yes!' Phil called out on the edge of the six-yard box and Raheem picked him out perfectly. He didn't have much room or time, so with his silky first touch, Phil shifted the ball to the left and then fired a quick shot at goal. Alisson dived down and saved it, but İlkay was there to smash home the rebound. *1–0 to City!*

'Yesssssssss!' Phil yelled, throwing both arms above

his head. Although he hadn't scored the goal himself, his clever movement had helped create it.

City's lead didn't last long, though. Mohamed Salah won a penalty and scored from the spot. *1–1 – game on!*

A draw at Anfield would be a decent result for City, but Phil wanted all three points to keep his team at the top of the Premier League table. So, could he create a moment of match-winning magic?

In the seventieth minute, Phil got the ball on the left and glided past Fabinho. The only way the Brazilian could stop him was to bring him down. *Free kick, yellow card!*

Then a few minutes later, Phil was over on the right when Alisson sliced a goal kick straight to him. As he controlled the ball, he wasn't far outside the Liverpool box, but he still had lots of work to do. With a burst of speed, Phil escaped in between Jordan Henderson and Andrew Robertson, and kept dribbling into the six-yard box. Looking up, Phil could see İlkay and Raheem waiting in the middle, but how was he going to get the ball across to them? Alisson and Fabinho were both standing tall in front of him, trying to block the way!

Phil, however, had spotted the smallest of gaps and with the outside of his left boot, he poked the ball in between the two Liverpool players to pick out İlkay. *2–1!*

The touch, the balance, the skill and then the pass – unbelievable! Although the players all ran over to celebrate with İlkay the goalscorer, Phil was the real City hero.

'That was magic!' Raheem told Phil as they stood together in the big team hug.

From that moment on, City were absolutely unstoppable.

Another Alisson error fell to Bernardo, who crossed to Raheem. *3–1!*

Then with ten minutes to go, Phil got on the ball again and produced the best moment of the whole match. From wide on the right, he controlled it with the outside of his boot and dribbled straight at the Liverpool defence. Robertson did his best to stop him, but with a sudden drop of the shoulder, Phil shifted

the ball to the left to make space for the shot, and
BANG! The ball rocketed past Alisson before he could
really react, and into the roof of the net. *4–1!*

*Goooooooooooooooooooooaaaaaaaaaaaaaaaaalllllllllllllllll
llllllllllll!!!!!!!!!!!!!!!!!!!!!*

Phil turned and raced away with one arm in the
air, just like a real striker. Wow, what a hit – it was
one of the sweetest strikes of his life. Not bad for a
new false nine! As his teammates congratulated him
with hugs and high-fives, Phil's face broke out into
a beaming smile. It was a goal and a game that he
would never forget, another massive moment in his
big breakthrough season.

After that amazing win at Anfield, unstoppable City
stormed to their fifth Premier League title. Champions
again! Phil felt so proud to have played a much bigger
part for his team this time. With nine goals and five
assists, he had become one of Pep's most important
attackers and he was also named the Premier League
Young Player of the Season.

What a successful year Phil was having, and there
were still more trophies for him to win. In the League

Cup final against Tottenham, he once again played as City's false nine, and he almost grabbed another big-game goal. Midway through the first half, a clearance fell to him inside the six-yard box and in a flash he swept the ball towards the net. He was all ready to race away and celebrate, but his shot struck a Tottenham defender and then bounced off the post and wide.

Noooooooooo! Phil couldn't believe his bad luck. Eventually, however, City found a way to win, just like they had all season. Kevin curled a free kick into the box and Aymeric jumped the highest to head the ball in. *1–0!*

Yessssssssss, City were celebrating at Wembley once again! While their Quadruple dream was ended by Chelsea in the FA Cup semi-finals, they had done the Double and the Treble was still on:

League Cup? *Tick!*

Premier League title? *Tick!*

...And City were through to their first-ever Champions League final.

CHAPTER 21

A PAINFUL NIGHT IN PORTO

'Guys, this is going to be our year!' Pep had told his players back at the start of the season. After losing in the quarter-finals for the last three seasons in a row, City were going all the way in 2021, to hopefully win the Champions League at last.

That was the plan, and City had stuck to it. They finished top of their group without losing a single game, and then strolled past Borussia Mönchengladbach in the Round of 16.

'Another big performance,' Phil tweeted after a sensational turn and dribble to set up another goal for İlkay. He was really enjoying his latest European experience. 'Quarters here we come!'

The competition was about to get more difficult, though, because next up, City faced Borussia Dortmund. Sadly, Phil's friend Jadon missed both legs because of an injury, but the German giants still had lots of other star players: Marco Reus, Julian Brandt, Thorgan Hazard, and most dangerous of all, Erling Haaland. The Norwegian striker had scored ten goals in the Champions League already that season!

So, could City break their quarter-final curse and reach the semis at last? Fortunately, they had an amazing young attacker of their own. In the last minute of the first leg at the Etihad, Kevin whipped a long ball to the back post, where İlkay knocked it down for Phil to fire in the winner. *2–1!*

Goooooooooooooooooooaaaaaaaaaaaaaaaaallllllllllllll llllllllllll!!!!!!!!!!!!!!!!!!!

'Yessssssss, you hero!' İlkay cheered as he jumped on Phil's back.

In the second leg at the Westfalenstadion, Phil again scored the winner for City. From a corner, Bernardo found him in lots of space on the edge of the Dortmund box. Phil calmly took a touch to control and shift the ball out of his feet and then fired a shot that flew in off the post. *2–1!*

Goooooooooooooooooooooooaaaaaaaaaaaaaaaaalllllllllllllll llllllllllllll!!!!!!!!!!!!!!!!!!!!!!

After a quick check to make sure that the ball had gone in, Phil turned and raced over to the sidelines to celebrate with his manager who had always believed in him.

'You did it, I knew you could do it!' Pep yelled excitedly in his ear.

City were through to the Champions League semi-finals, and they had their phenomenal Number 47 to thank for that. Sometimes Phil had to pinch himself to make sure it wasn't all a dream.

'Hey, I'm the one who was supposed to score the goals!' Erling joked with him as they swapped shirts after the final whistle.

City had succeeded in keeping Haaland quiet, but could they do the same against Kylian Mbappé and Neymar Jr? That was their next big Champions League challenge. It wasn't easy, but in the end, they battled their way past PSG. Phil didn't score this time, but he still played a very important part in both matches.

Away in Paris, he won a free kick on the edge of the box, which Riyad curled through the wall and into the bottom corner. *2–1 to City!*

Then back home at the Etihad, Phil carried the ball forward from his own half on a lightning counter-attack. After playing a one-two with Kevin, Phil looked up and slid a perfect pass across to Riyad at the back post. *2–0 to City!*

Phil almost added a magnificent third goal of his own moments later. As the ball came towards him, he had his back to the PSG goal, but he somehow managed to control it and spin all in one beautiful movement. Wow, forget Mbappé and Neymar Jr; Phil was the star of the show in the Champions League semi-final at the Parc de Princes! He glided away from Presnel Kimpembe and unleashed a powerful low strike, but the ball clipped the outside of the post. *So unlucky!*

Never mind, it didn't really matter because City were through to their first-ever Champions League final! The players allowed themselves a small celebration on the pitch afterwards, but they weren't getting carried away. They hadn't won the trophy yet...

Their opponents in the final would be their English rivals Chelsea, who had recently beaten them 1–0 in the FA Cup semi-final. 1–0? Yes, that's right, City hadn't been able to score a single goal! Under new manager Thomas Tuchel, the Chelsea defence had become almost impossible to break through, so would Pep make changes for the Champions League final?

Yes, he would – at the Dragão Stadium in Porto, City lined up without a single defensive midfielder. No Rodri, no Fernandinho; just İlkay, Bernardo... and Phil. Unbelievable – on the day after his twenty-first birthday, he was starting in the Champions League final!

'I've been dreaming about this moment since I was five years old,' Phil reminded himself as he walked out past the trophy without even looking at it. It was the biggest game of his life, and the fans were back to watch it live. COVID-19 rules meant only

14,000 supporters were allowed in the stadium, but it sounded like a lot more. 'Listen to that noise – it's my time to shine!'

It was a bold move from Pep to select such an attacking midfield, and unfortunately, it backfired. City passed and moved, passed and moved, but despite all their possession, they weren't making much progress. N'Golo Kanté and Jorginho were winning almost everything in midfield and if City did manage to get past them, there was always a Chelsea defender in the way.

Raheem raced onto Ederson's long goal kick, but Reece James tracked back to make the tackle.

Raheem crossed the ball towards Riyad at the back post, but Ben Chilwell slid in to intercept it.

Phil burst into the box, but just as he went to shoot, Antonio Rüdiger made a brilliant block.

Then, right at the end of the first half, Chelsea counter-attacked with two quick passes and Kai Havertz raced through to score. *1–0!*

Nooooooooo! Phil couldn't believe it. If only he had taken his chance...

City worked hard in the second half to turn things around, but sadly, it just wasn't their lucky night. First Kevin had to go off with a fractured nose, and then Raheem's shot appeared to hit James on the arm, but the referee said, 'No penalty!'

City kept going, hoping the goal would come. Phil dribbled forward and passed it wide to Riyad, who crossed it in towards İlkay... ball cleared again!

Riyad pulled it back to Phil on the edge of the six-yard box... shot blocked again!

Moments later, it was all over and Chelsea were the new Champions of Europe. As he heard the whistle blow, Phil fell to the floor, exhausted and heartbroken. City had come so close to lifting the trophy, but they had fallen at the final hurdle.

In a daze of disappointment, Phil walked around shaking hands with all the Chelsea players and then went up to collect his runners-up medal. He didn't wear it proudly around his neck. No, he would only do that once it was a winner's medal and City were the Champions of Europe.

CHAPTER 22

EURO 2020

Fortunately, Phil soon had something new to look forward to. Just three days after that painful night in Porto, Gareth Southgate picked his final twenty-six players for the delayed Euro 2020 competition:

'Forwards: Dominic Calvert-Lewin (Everton), Phil Foden (Manchester City)...'

Yessss, he was in! Back in 2018, Phil had travelled to Russia to watch England play at the World Cup; now, three years later, he would be playing for them at a major tournament. Unbelievable, what a journey!

'A massive honour to be a part of the England squad for the Euros,' Phil tweeted as he arrived at St George's Park. 'Time to get to work.'

After a hard day's work on the training field, there was time for fun too – Fifa, Fortnite, yoga, swimming, darts, basketball, and even a visit to the barbers. Phil walked into the England camp with the same brown hairstyle he'd had for years, but a few days later, he decided to do something different – he dyed it blond! Why? 'Euro 96 vibes,' he explained on his Instagram story.

Phil hadn't even been born when that tournament took place, but he had seen all the highlights on TV, especially Paul Gascoigne's stunning strike against Scotland. The maverick midfielder had bleached his hair blond for Euro 96, and so Phil thought maybe he could bring a bit of Gazza on the pitch at Euro 2020.

'And if we go all the way and win it, you all have to get the same haircut as me!' he told the other England players, who reluctantly agreed. Why not?!

With the squad spending so much time together on and off the football pitch, the team spirit was stronger than ever. Phil was already close with Kyle, John and Raheem from City, plus Jadon of course, but he also became good friends with Jack Grealish, Bukayo

Saka, and Declan Rice. Everyone got on really well, no matter how old they were or what club team they played for. For the next few weeks, they were all on the same team, working together to win the same trophy.

But what would England's starting line-up be? There was so much competition for places all over the pitch, and especially in attack. There was only really one spot up for grabs in Southgate's first-choice front-three. It would be Harry, Raheem, and who???

Raheem preferred to play on the left side, so it was a right winger that England needed. That was Jadon's best position, where he could attack with speed and skill. But perhaps Southgate would go for something different instead:

A creative playmaker like Phil or Jack,

A proper goalscorer like Marcus,

Or an energetic all-rounder like Bukayo?

The England manager had so many excellent options to choose from, each with a different style and different strengths. He was going to have some very difficult decisions to make.

For their first match against Croatia, Southgate went for... Phil! It was a dream come true for Phil to be playing for his country in such an important game, and his Euro experience almost got off to the perfect start. In only the sixth minute, Raheem dribbled forward and slipped it right to Phil as he entered the box. What a chance! His heart was really racing, but Phil kept calm, cut inside on his left foot, and then *BANG!* His shot flew past the keeper, and curled towards the far bottom corner... but no, it hit the post. *So close!*

Phil kept going, looking for another chance to score, but in the end, Raheem was the England hero. Racing onto a great pass from Kalvin Phillips, he took his shot straight away, firing past the keeper and into the net. *1–0!*

Phil raced over to the corner flag to join the celebrations, high-fiving Kalvin along the way. England were winning!

'Raz, you're on fire!' he shouted, hugging his City teammate tightly.

After seventy minutes of silky touches and non-stop

movement, Phil left the field to a standing ovation from the Wembley crowd. He just hoped he'd be back for the next match; he was enjoying every moment at Euro 2020.

With that 1–0 win, England moved on to a big local derby against British rivals, Scotland. Wait a minute, Scotland, that goal at Euro 96 – surely, they were going to want their new Gazza on the pitch? Yes, for the second game in a row, Southgate named Phil in the starting line-up!

Despite all the excitement surrounding the game, however, it ended up being a disappointing 0–0 draw, especially for Phil. He started brightly, just like he had against Croatia, but he struggled to find that killer final pass or shot, that much-needed moment of magic. So, in the sixtieth minute, Southgate took him off and brought on Jack instead.

Oh dear, was this to be the end of Phil's Euro 2020 experience? It certainly looked that way when he didn't play in the 1–0 win over the Czech Republic...

...Or their 2–0 victory against Germany in the Round of 16...

...Or their 4–0 thrashing of Ukraine in the quarter-finals.

Phil wanted to be out on the pitch playing for his country, of course, but he was still young and he was still learning at senior international level. Plus, there were lots of other amazing attackers in the squad. So instead of sulking, Phil supported his teammates from the subs bench and ran over to celebrate each goal. The main thing was that England were winning, and they were through to the Euro semi-finals!

Next up: Denmark. Phil started on the bench again, but with the game tied at 1–1 in extra-time, England needed more energy and creativity. So off went Mason Mount and on he came! It felt so good to be back on the pitch, but could he make a big-game impact with a moment of magic?

As Raheem dribbled his way into the box, Phil was waiting in a pocket of space, ready to receive the pass. But instead, Raheem kept going, past one Denmark defender, and as he glided past another, he was barged in the side.

'PENALTY!' Phil cried out with both arms in the air,

and the referee pointed straight to the spot.

So, could Harry fire England into the Euro 2020 final? His spot-kick was saved, but he scored the rebound. *2–1!*

'YESSSSSSSSSSSSS!' As his captain slid towards the corner flag on his knees, Phil was right behind him, followed by all of their teammates. What a moment – for the first time since 1966, England were going through to the final of a major tournament!

'I can't believe we've made it!' Phil shouted in Jack's ear as the celebrations went on long after the final whistle at Wembley, both on the pitch and in the stands.

'It's coming home, it's coming home,
It's coming, FOOTBALL'S COMING HOME!'

SWEET CAROLINE! Da-da-daa
Good times never seemed so good
So good, so good, so good!'

'WHAT A FEELING,' Phil posted later that night,

with the adrenaline still buzzing through his body.
'LETS GOOOOOO!!!'

England were now only one game away from glory,
and Phil was desperate to play a part in the final. Back
in 2017, he had scored two goals in the Under-17
World Cup final – hopefully, he could become a
national hero again!

Two days before the big match, however, Phil hurt
his foot in training. At first, the injury didn't seem too
serious, but would the pain go away in time for him to
play? Eventually, the England manager had to make a
very difficult decision.

'I'm really sorry, but I'm going to have to leave you
out of the squad for the final.'

As Southgate gave him the bad news, Phil burst
out crying. He couldn't help it; he was absolutely
devastated to be missing the biggest match of his life.
Yes, he probably would have been on the bench to
start with, but he could have been England's super
sub!

Phil was a real team player, though, and so as the
Euro 2020 final kicked off at Wembley, he was there

on the sidelines, wearing his England tracksuit with pride and supporting his friends.

'Yesssssss!' he cheered as Luke Shaw scored in the second minute. *1–0!*

'Nooooooo!' he groaned as Leonardo Bonucci equalised for Italy. *1–1!*

As the goal went in, Phil had a horrible feeling about where the match was heading: PENALTIES! And he was right – arghhh, he could hardly bear to watch. While he really wished he could be out there helping his team, Phil believed in England's penalty takers. They could do this...

1) Harry Kane... SCORED!

Yesssssss!

2) Harry Maguire... SCORED!

Yesssssss!

3) Marcus... HIT THE POST!

Noooooo!

4) Jadon aimed for the bottom corner and... SAVED!

Noooooo!

The final wasn't over yet, though. Jordan Pickford

made a super save to keep out Jorginho's penalty, which meant that England could equalise if they scored their last spot-kick...

5) Bukayo went for the same bottom corner as Jadon and... SAVED AGAIN!

NOOOOO!

Now it really was over – England had lost, and Italy were the Euro 2020 winners. As he made his way out onto the pitch, Phil felt distraught, but he pushed his own emotions to the side because he knew how much his teammates would be hurting.

'Bro, you were so brave to even take that,' he said, hugging Jadon tightly. 'Remember, we win together, we lose together, and we'll be back – the World Cup's coming up next year!'

CHAPTER 23

BACK AND BETTER THAN EVER!

First the Champions League and now Euro 2020 – it was Phil's second defeat in a major final in just six weeks. That was a lot of disappointment for a young player to deal with. Perhaps it was time for him to take a break and enjoy some fun in the sun, or even a relaxing fishing trip with his dad...

But when City offered him a holiday, Phil said no. He didn't want a rest; what he wanted was to start physio on his foot straight away, so that he could get himself fit for the new season. The defeats against Chelsea and Italy had only made him even more determined to succeed.

'Boss, I'm going to come back better than ever!' he

promised Pep.

Phil's recovery felt frustratingly slow, but by October 2021, he was finally flying again for club and country.

Away at Anfield, Phil was electric once more, causing all kinds of trouble for the Liverpool right-back, James Milner. The speed, the skill, the movement – he was just so hard to mark! He should have had a penalty in the first half, and in the second, he found more space on the left and calmly fired a low shot past Alisson.

Goooooooooooooooooooooaaaaaaaaaaaaaaaalllllllllllll lllllllllll!!!!!!!!!!!!!!!!!!

'Come onnnnn!' Phil yelled, urging his City teammates on. He was back with a bang!

A week later, he was off on international duty, dazzling for England. Against Andorra, Phil ran the game from the middle of midfield, showing off his incredible creativity.

He chipped a beautiful ball over the top to Jadon, who passed to Ben Chilwell. 1–0!

He curled a defence-splitting pass through to Bukayo, who finished in style. 2–0!

Was there anything the wonderkid couldn't do?!
Attack or midfield; on the left, on the right, or in the
middle – it didn't really matter what position Phil
played. His pure quality shone brightly anywhere on
the pitch.

In the Champions League against Club Brugge,
Phil was City's false nine, but he had the freedom to
roam around as he pleased. In the thirtieth minute,
he dropped deep to collect the ball, looked up and
delivered an exceptional, inch-perfect pass to João.
1–0!

On the sidelines, Pep jumped up out of his seat,
smiling and pointing at Phil, as if to say, 'You – you are
a very special player!'

Match after match, he was making a difference for
City:

Two goals and an assist against Brighton,

A wonderful cross to Raheem against Watford,

A stunning side-foot volley to beat Brentford…

With Phil back and better than ever, City looked
unstoppable again. He helped his team to finish first
above PSG in their Champions League group and

climb their way to the top of the Premier League table too. What would City do without their home-grown hero?

He's one of our own,
He's one of our own,
Ohhhh Phil Foden he's one of our own!

Wow, it still gave him goosebumps to hear the fans sing his name. At the age of twenty-one, Phil was living his dream and living up to his huge potential. Through hard work and dedication, the little boy from Stockport had grown up to become a City and England superstar, as well as one of the best young players on the planet. Yes, Mbappé, Haaland, and Foden – the future of football was theirs.

Continue for a sneak preview of
another brilliant football story by
Matt and Tom Oldfield. . .

DAVID SILVA

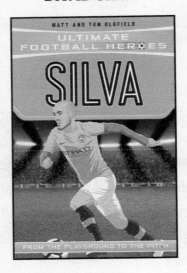

Available now!

CHAPTER 1

CITY'S GREATEST

22 April 2018, Etihad Stadium, Manchester

After shaking hands with the Swansea City players, David took off his tracksuit top and got ready for action. Jumping and shouting wasn't really his style; instead, he walked onto the pitch with a calm, quiet confidence.

'We're going to win today,' David thought to himself, 'and we're going to do it in style!'

His team, Manchester City, were the new Premier League Champions, and the players couldn't wait to celebrate that achievement in front of a heaving home crowd. First, they would play another ninety minutes of fantastic football, and then they would lift the trophy. There would be plenty for the fans to cheer about:

CITY! CITY! CITY!

There was a party atmosphere in the stadium, but David was in no mood to relax. He wanted to be on the ball as often as possible, creating moments of magic for his team. Pass and move, pass and move, pass and move – that was the new City way under their amazing manager, Pep Guardiola.

The football was fast and flowing; a joy to watch and even greater joy to play. Kevin De Bruyne slid the ball through to Raheem Sterling, who pulled it back to David. The pass was slightly behind him, but he didn't panic. No, David just flicked the ball up and then volleyed it past the goalkeeper. *1–0!*

Goooooooooooooooooooooooooooooaaaaaaaaaaaaaaa aaaaaaaaallllllllllllllllllllllllllllllllllll!!!!!!!!!!!!!!!!!!!!

'Nice one, mate!' Raheem said, putting an arm around his shoulder.

The City show had started with another great team goal. David ran towards the fans with his right arm raised in the air and the thumb of his left hand in his mouth. He was dedicating the goal to his sick son, Mateo. He was always in David's thoughts, even out on the football pitch. Hopefully, Mateo would be out of the hospital soon, and then he would get to watch his dad play.

'One day!' David told himself.

After that special moment, he settled back into central midfield to play his favourite role: pass-master. That's where Pep wanted him to be, running the game for City with his remarkable touch and vision. David loved his deeper role because he had more time and space to work his magic.

'Here!' he called for the ball again and again.

David was always available, and he was always thinking one step ahead. Who should he pass to next? Could he spot anyone making a brilliant run?

Fifteen minutes in, and the Swansea players already felt like giving up. How were they supposed to win the ball back from midfield maestros like David and Kevin? They passed and passed but they never made mistakes – ever! They were just too good and soon, it was game over.

Fabian Delph to David, David back to Fabian,
Fabian across to Raheem. 2–0!

City's superstars celebrated with a big group hug.
Their Premier League title party was going exactly
according to plan.

'Nice finish!' said David.

'Nice cross!' said Raheem.

'Nice pass!' said Fabian.

In the second half, City went searching for
more. They were never satisfied, and neither were
their fans. They had come to see goals, and plenty
of them.

Kevin hit a long-range rocket. *3–0!*

David got the ball, turned beautifully and played an
unbelievable pass through to Raheem. As he went to
shoot, a defender fouled him. *Penalty!* Gabriel Jesus
missed the spot-kick, but Bernardo Silva scored the
rebound. *4–0!*

Yaya Touré chipped a ball over the top for Gabriel to
head home. *5–0!*

What a season City were having! That was their
ninety-eighth goal in only thirty-five Premier League

games. They were now just five goals behind the all-time record, with four games still to go.

'We want six! We want six!' their supporters cheered merrily.

Five would do just fine, though. Job done! At the final whistle, the City players went off and then came back on wearing special shirts with '18 CHAMPIONS' on the back. One by one, they were called up to collect their winners' medals.

Number 31, Ederson...

...Number 17, Kevin De Bruyne...

...Number 10, Manchester City's all-time record goalscorer, Sergio Agüero!

The cheers got louder and louder until there were only two players left: City's two legendary leaders. Vincent Kompany, the club captain would go last, but first...

Number 21, 'El Mago', The Magician, DAVID SILVA!

When he walked up onto the stage, he waved modestly to the screaming supporters. Without a football at his feet, David didn't feel so comfortable in front of so many people. Still, he had a smile on his face as he joined his teammates. It was almost time for the big moment.

Oooooooooooooo...

Vincent gathered everyone around him and then lifted the Premier League trophy high into the sky.

...Hurraaaaaaaaay!

It was a good thing that David never got tired of that winning feeling. He had won three major tournaments with Spain – Euro 2008, World Cup 2010 and Euro 2012 – and now seven major competitions with City – one FA Cup, three League Cups and three Premier League titles. That was a whole lot of winning and yet the celebrations were still as exciting as ever.

At last, David held the trophy in his hands. As he raised it above his head, he could hear the supporters singing:

He came from Spain with just one aim – SILVA! SILVA!

He came to make us great again, SILVA! SILVA!

When his job with us was done,

And all the trophies he had won,
We called him David Silva – CITY'S KING OF
SPAIN!

Sergio scored lots of goals, Vincent was a rock at the back, but was David their greatest-ever player? The City fans certainly seemed to think so. He had changed their club forever. They had so much love and respect for 'The Magician of Arguineguín'.

CHAPTER 2

ANY BALL, ANY PITCH

'Come on, let's go out and play!' David cried out impatiently.

Like most days in Arguineguín, it was way too hot to be stuck indoors all day. The Canary Islands were part of Spain, but they were actually much nearer to the North-west coast of Africa. Although all the windows in the house were wide open, even that couldn't cool them down. It was much better to be out at the beach, with the cool ocean breeze on their faces, and a football at their feet.

'But we don't have a ball anymore,' Ranzel, his cousin, explained. 'Remember, José kicked it into the sea and the tide took it away!'

'Hey, it was a shot! If you were a better goalkeeper, maybe you'd have saved it...'

As the others argued, David tried to think of a clever plan. What else could they use instead? A stone? A bottle? A scrunched-up newspaper? Any ball would do...A-ha! He had a great idea.

'Right, you wait here and keep watch,' he told his cousins. 'If you hear Grandma coming, make lots of noise, okay?'

'Okay!'

David was the youngest of the gang, but he was also the bravest. And now that he was nearly six years old, he was allowed to go out and play a little further away than just the alley at the side of their house. As long as Ranzel was there to keep an eye on him, they could set off on fun football adventures. But first, they would need to find a new ball.

After taking a long, deep breath, David crept quietly into the kitchen and tiptoed over to the cupboards. He opened the doors slowly, so that they wouldn't make a loud creaking sound.

Phew, he was in! So, what could he see? David

knew exactly what he was looking for. It was his grandmother who had first given him the idea of playing football using fruit. She often looked after her grandchildren, while their parents were out at work. And whenever David and his cousins were making too much noise inside the house, she would throw a potato or an orange into the alley, as if they were dogs chasing a bone.

'You can play out there until you quieten down a bit,' she would tell them. 'You're driving me mad with all that shouting about football!'

So, could David find a potato in the cupboard? Or a grapefruit? Or a melon? Any ball would do... A-ha – a bag of big, juicy oranges!

'Perfect!' he smiled to himself as he took two and put one in each pocket of his shorts. They would need a back-up ball, in case the first one burst.

They knew that they weren't allowed to take anything from the kitchen cupboards, but how would their grandmother ever know? There were still plenty of oranges left.

'Let's go out and play!' David called to the

others and they followed him out onto the streets
of Arguineguín.

The name meant 'quiet water' and that was a very
suitable description for it. The small fishing village was
a very safe and peaceful place for young kids to play.
Everyone knew everyone in Arguineguín. Now that
they had a ball, they just needed a football pitch. Any
ball, any pitch! There wasn't much grass around, so
where else could they play?

'Last one to the beach has to go in goal!' David
shouted as he sprinted into the lead.

The beach was where all Canary Islanders learnt
to play football. That was why they were so good at
the beautiful game; almost as good as the Brazilians!
It was hard work running up and down the bumpy
sand, especially while kicking a ball at the same time.
But luckily, David was a natural. The ball – or fruit
– always stayed stuck to his foot as he glided past
his cousins' tackles. He was the boy with the golden
touch. Not only was he the bravest, but he was also
the best at football.

'I'm on David's team!'

'No way, that's not fair. You'll thrash us!'

When they were old enough, David let his sister Natalia and his brother Nando join the football gang, but only on one condition:

'First, you've got to go get us a new "football"!'

For a long time, they thought they'd got away with their fruit-stealing tricks. They thought they were so clever, finding new 'footballs' whenever they needed them!

But then one day, David's dad gave him a special gift – a new football, made out of old cloths and rags. David's eyes grew wide with excitement. He couldn't wait to show his cousins.

'Wow, this is the best present ever. Thanks, Dad!'

Fernando laughed. 'My pleasure. At least now our kitchen cupboards will be safe!'

PHIL FODEN HONOURS

Manchester City

🏆 Premier League: 2017–18, 2018–19, 2020–21

🏆 FA Cup: 2018–19

🏆 EFL Cup: 2017–18, 2018–19, 2019–20,
2020–21

England Under-17s

🏆 FIFA U-17 World Cup: 2017

Individual

🏆 FIFA U-17 World Cup Golden Ball: 2017

🏆 BBC Young Sports Personality of the Year: 2017

🏆 Alan Hardaker Trophy for Man of the Match in the League Cup final: 2020

🏆 Premier League Young Player of the Season: 2020–21

🏆 PFA Young Player of the Year: 2020–21

FODEN

47 THE FACTS

NAME: Philip Walter Foden

DATE OF BIRTH: 28 May 2000

PLACE OF BIRTH: Stockport

NATIONALITY: English

BEST FRIENDS: Jadon Sancho and Jack Grealish

CURRENT CLUB: Manchester City

POSITION: LW/CAM

THE STATS

Height (cm):	171
Club appearances:	151
Club goals:	40
Club assists:	41
Club trophies:	8
International appearances:	13
International goals:	2
International trophies:	1
Ballon d'Ors:	0

★ ★ ★ **HERO RATING: 85** ★ ★ ★

GREATEST MOMENTS

28 OCTOBER 2017, ENGLAND 5–2 SPAIN

From 2–1 down at half-time, the England Under-17s bounced back brilliantly to beat Spain and win the World Cup final. With Jadon Sancho back at Borussia Dortmund, it was Phil who stepped up to lead the Young Lions to victory. He was the best player on the pitch in the second half, creating lots of chances and scoring two great goals. Phil even won the Golden Ball award for the best player at the tournament.

1 MARCH 2020, ASTON VILLA 1–2 MANCHESTER CITY

This was Phil's third League Cup final, but his first in the City starting line-up. With the chance to play the full ninety minutes, he really made the most of it. Phil headed the ball across to Sergio Agüero to set up City's first goal, and he was their stand-out player all game long. At the final whistle, he got the Man of the Match award, to go with his winner's medal and the League Cup trophy.

18 NOVEMBER 2020, ENGLAND 4–0 ICELAND

This was the night when Phil became an England hero again. He had been sent home for bad behaviour after his senior international debut, but now he was ready to make it up to his manager Gareth Southgate. First, he set up Declan Rice with a dangerous free kick, and then he scored two goals of his own in the second half.

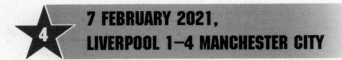

4 7 FEBRUARY 2021, LIVERPOOL 1–4 MANCHESTER CITY

This was Phil's best performance during his breakthrough season at City. Playing in a false nine role, he was electric against their big rivals, Liverpool. He helped create the first goal with his clever movement, set up the second for İlkay Gündoğan with a perfect pass, and then scored the fourth himself with a stunning strike. Soon, City were Premier League Champions again.

5 6 APRIL 2021, MANCHESTER CITY 2–1 BORUSSIA DORTMUND

Could City finally break their Champions League curse and reach the semi-finals? In the quarters, they faced Dortmund and their star striker, Erling Haaland. He had already scored ten goals in the tournament, but he wasn't the match-winning hero this time. That was Phil! In the last minute, he stayed calm and swept the ball past the keeper. In the second leg, Phil scored the winner again, to take City into the Champions League semi-finals at last.

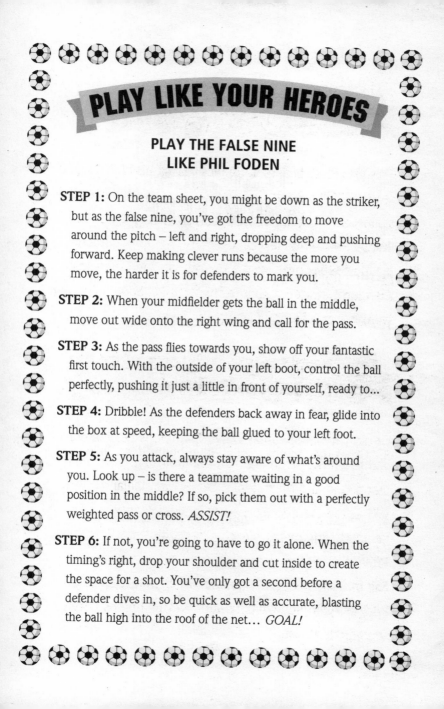

PLAY LIKE YOUR HEROES

PLAY THE FALSE NINE
LIKE PHIL FODEN

STEP 1: On the team sheet, you might be down as the striker, but as the false nine, you've got the freedom to move around the pitch – left and right, dropping deep and pushing forward. Keep making clever runs because the more you move, the harder it is for defenders to mark you.

STEP 2: When your midfielder gets the ball in the middle, move out wide onto the right wing and call for the pass.

STEP 3: As the pass flies towards you, show off your fantastic first touch. With the outside of your left boot, control the ball perfectly, pushing it just a little in front of yourself, ready to...

STEP 4: Dribble! As the defenders back away in fear, glide into the box at speed, keeping the ball glued to your left foot.

STEP 5: As you attack, always stay aware of what's around you. Look up – is there a teammate waiting in a good position in the middle? If so, pick them out with a perfectly weighted pass or cross. *ASSIST!*

STEP 6: If not, you're going to have to go it alone. When the timing's right, drop your shoulder and cut inside to create the space for a shot. You've only got a second before a defender dives in, so be quick as well as accurate, blasting the ball high into the roof of the net... *GOAL!*

TEST YOUR KNOWLEDGE

QUESTIONS

1. What nickname did Phil get from his grandmother, and why?

2. Who first predicted that Phil would play for England one day?

3. Other than football, what other hobby does Phil share with his dad?

4. For the Manchester derby, which members of the Foden family supported which team?

5. True or false – Phil was there when Manchester City first won the Premier League in 2012.

6. In 2017, Phil was seen as one of Manchester City's three most promising young players – who were the other two?

7. Which nation did Phil's England Under-17s lose to in the Euros final, but then beat in the World Cup final a few months later?

8. How old was Phil when he made his debut for the Manchester City first-team?

9. Which Manchester City player did Phil call 'The Master' because he learned so much from him?

10. Phil set up City's first goal in the 2020 League Cup final against Aston Villa, but who scored it?

11. What colour did Phil dye his hair for Euro 2020, and why?

1. 'Ronnie' because he was born with a head that looked like a football, a 'Ronnie Roundhead'. 2. His grandfather, Walter. 3. Fishing. 4. Phil Sr and Callum supported United, while Phil Jr and Claire supported City. 5. True – he was sitting behind the goal where Sergio Agüero scored the last-minute winner. 6. Jadon Sancho and Brahim Díaz. 7. Spain. 8. 17 (17 years and 177 days to be exact!). 9. David Silva. 10. Sergio Agüero. 11. He dyed it blond because a) he felt like a change and b) Gazza had done it for Euro 96.

CAN'T GET ENOUGH OF ULTIMATE FOOTBALL HEROES?

**Check out heroesfootball.com
for quizzes, games, and competitions!**

**Plus join the Ultimate Football Heroes
Fan Club to score exclusive content
and be the first to hear about
new books and events.
heroesfootball.com/subscribe/**